RUIN *the*
SACRED
TRUTHS

The Charles Eliot Norton

Lectures 1987–88

the Argument

Held me a while misdoubting his Intent,

That he would ruin (for I saw him strong)

The sacred Truths to Fable and Old Song

Andrew Marvell, "On *Paradise Lost*"

Harvard University Press

Cambridge, Massachusetts, and London, England

RUIN *the*

SACRED

TRUTHS

&. *Poetry and Belief* &.

from the Bible to the Present

HAROLD BLOOM

First Harvard University Press paperback edition, 1991

Library of Congress Catalog Number 88-021651

ISBN 0-674-78027-2 (alk. paper) (cloth)
ISBN 0-674-78028-0 (paper)

Designed by Gwen Frankfeldt

For Jonathan Spence

Preface

This book consists of an expanded text of the 1987–88 Charles
Eliot Norton Lectures at Harvard University.

I am grateful to Marjorie Garber, Kathryne Lindberg,
Robert and Jana Kiely, Cresap and Sally Moore, Lucy Boling,
Victoria Macy, Edison Miyawaki, and Betty McNally for
the kindness of their hospitality during the academic year
1987–88.

Harold Bloom
Cambridge, Massachusetts
March 1988

I

THE HEBREW BIBLE 1

II

FROM HOMER TO DANTE 25

III

SHAKESPEARE 51

IV

MILTON 89

V

ENLIGHTENMENT AND
ROMANTICISM 115

VI

FREUD AND BEYOND 143

RUIN *the*
SACRED
TRUTHS

I

THE
HEBREW
BIBLE

&

S OMEWHERE about the year 100 B.C.E., a Pharisee composed what tradition has called the Book of Jubilees, an exuberant title for quite a bad piece of writing. This garrulous work is also known as the Little Genesis, an odd naming since it is much longer than Genesis and covers Exodus as well. I don't enjoy reading the Book of Jubilees, but it fascinates me, not by anything it contains, but by everything it excludes. What it leaves out of Genesis and Exodus, by a curiously proleptic design, is very nearly everything in those books of the Hebrew Bible that modern scholarship has assigned to the authorship of the Yahwist, or J writer. Let us call him simply J, and muse at his virtual expulsion from this Pharasaic retelling.

J, according to a number of current Biblical scholars, including many literalists who refuse to recognize a metaphor even when it confronts them, has had no real existence, but merely was invented by the Wellhausen school and those who came after. Authorship is somewhat out of fashion at the moment, because of Parisian preferences, but like shorter skirts authorship always does return again. I am not going to argue with theory on this, since I believe that literature is part of speculation or wonder, and any hypothesis is good enough for me. American criticism, as Richard Rorty spendidly reminds us, is one of the consequences of pragmatism. The primal author J, more ancient than his great rival, the hypothesis Homer, constitutes a difference that has made an overwhelming difference, overdetermining all of us—Jew, Christian, Muslim, and secularist. J told stories, so did Homer. One cannot award the palm for narrative strength to one over the other. All any of us can say is that Genesis and Exodus, the *Iliad* and the *Odyssey*, establish literary strength or the sublime, and then we estimate

Dante and Chaucer, Cervantes and Shakespeare, Tolstoy and Proust against that standard of measurement.

There are no two strong authors more unlike than J and Homer. I write that, and then I have to reflect that Tolstoy resembles both, professedly by design. But he resembles different elements in each. *War and Peace* and, even more, *Hadji Murad,* the short novel in which the aged Tolstoy returned to the military theater of his youth, give us something close to the Homeric sense of men in battle, with the shifting movement between individual combat and group warfare. They exclude Homer's gods, and the Homeric strife between gods and men. What they share with the Yahwist, implicitly, is the cosmos governed by Yahweh, in which an ultimate trust is possible. What they exclude of J is a radical irony, unlike almost any other, that I find also in certain moments of Kafka. This irony is neither the contrast or gap between expectation and fulfillment, nor the saying of one thing while meaning quite another. It is the irony of J's Hebraic sublime, in which absolutely incommensurate realities collide and cannot be resolved.

To represent Yahweh at all is the largest instance of such sublime irony, and raises permanently the unresolvable aesthetic issue of poetry and belief. I myself do not believe that secularization is itself a literary process. The scandal is the stubborn resistance of imaginative literature to the categories of sacred and secular. If you wish, you can insist that all high literature is secular, or, should you desire it so, then all strong poetry is sacred. What I find incoherent is the judgment that some authentic literary art is more sacred or more secular than some other. Poetry and belief wander about, together and apart, in a cosmological emptiness marked by the limits of truth and of meaning. Somewhere between truth and meaning can be found piled up a terrible heap of descriptions of God. I do not recall ever reading an attempt, by a Biblical scholar or literary critic, to describe precisely *how* J went about giving us a representation of Yahweh. It is quite possible that J created Yahweh, even though J did not invent him. The representations of Yahweh by the Elohist, or by the Priestly writer, or by the Deuteronomist, or by the prophets: all these differ immensely from J's vision of God. "Vision of God" is not an accurate phrase to apply to J's mode of representing Yahweh, since his images of Yahweh are not visual but auditive, dynamic, and motor. But just as J's Jacob or J's Tamar is a superb personality, so is J's Yahweh, though "personality" is a surprising word to employ in this context. Surprise, however, is one of the dominant elements of J's Yahweh. This first Yahweh, so different from his shrunken form in normative Judaism and Christianity, is the crown of J's work, and remains impossible for us to assimilate, at least without a spiritual and cognitive crisis throughout our culture, even among the most secular.

A crisis, particularly of a cognitive kind, need be no more than a crossing point, a turning or troping that takes you down a path that proves to be rather more your own than you could have anticipated. I think my true subject, as a critic, has been what traditionally was called the sublime, which I would describe—following the ancient we call Longinus, as well as Shelley in his *Defence of Poetry*—as the mode of literary agon, the struggle on the part of every person to answer the triple question concerning the contending forces of past and present: more? equal to? or less than? Longinus and Shelley also imply that the literary sublime is the reader's sublime, which means that the reader must be able to defer pleasure, yielding up easier satisfactions in favor of a more delayed and difficult reward. That difficulty is an authentic mark of originality, an originality that must seem eccentric until it usurps psychic space and establishes itself as a fresh center. This is an ancient theory of poetry, older even than Longinus, because it goes back to Aristophanes' account, in *The Frogs*, of the agon between Aeschylus and Euripides, where Euripides manifests all the symptoms of a severe case of the anxiety of influence.

I began to arrive at the idea I am calling by the manufactured word "facticity" when I carefully reread the great original of all the authors in the Hebrew Bible. J's stories of Yahweh and the Patriarchs are so familiar to us that we simply cannot read them, because they are uncanny or sublime in Freud's sense of the *unheimlich,* something too familiar. These stories remain so original that we cannot read them in quite another sense, which is that we are still part of a tradition that has never been able to assimilate their originality, despite many efforts to do so. I am thinking of such weird tales as Yahweh making Adam by scooping up some wet clay and then breathing upon it, or Yahweh sitting upon the ground under the terebinths at Mamre, devouring roast calf, curd, milk and bread, and then being offended by the aged Sarah's sensible derision when he prophesies the birth of Isaac. But there are uncannier tales of Yahweh that J tells us, such as Yahweh's impish behavior when he confounds the bold builders of the tower of Babel; Yahweh's murderous and unmotivated attack on Moses in Exodus, when poor Moses has camped at night on the way down to Egypt; and the extraordinary story of Yahweh burying Moses, with his own hands, in an unmarked grave. More extraordinary even is the story J tells, not of Yahweh, but of an angel whom I interpret as being the angel of death, a nameless one with whom Jacob wrestles all night at Penuel in order to win the agonistic blessing of the new name that is Israel. That these stories, and others like them, cannot be dismissed as anthropomorphic and cannot be rendered merely normative is analytically quite demonstrable, but I have cited as mere historical evidence that every crucial trace of the J writer has been totally erased from the Book of Jubilees, whose highly normative author simply refused to assimilate everything about J that is most original and difficult.

J was a vastly eccentric great writer whose difficulty and originality are still obscured for us, and by us, because of a condition of enclosure that J's force has imposed upon us. When we attempt to call J's stories of Yahweh anthropomorphic, we truly are defending ourselves against J, by over-literalizing the figurative being he called Yahweh. When that over-literalization reaches its final point, then you end up with what Blake satirized as our vision of God as Urizen or No-bodaddy, a cloudy old man hovering up in the sky. Yet, in the Sinai Theophany, J shows us a picnic scene, Moses and seventy elders of Israel sitting and eating a Covenant meal while staring directly at Yahweh. Faced by the uncanny dignity of what we might call theomorphic Patriarchs as represented by J, we retreat into the mere facticity of muttering about an anthropomorphic deity.

The two other major instances of this imprisoning facticity are Shakespeare and Freud, in the sense that E. P. Thompson, the English Marxist historian, called Shakespeare "the old Adam of the English idiom," and in the more recent sense in which Freud has usurped our diction for describing all psychic instances, agencies, and events. By "facticity" I mean the state of being caught up in a factuality or contingency which is an inescapable and unalterable context. I do *not* mean a facticity in Heidegger's sense, because his hermeneutic privileges Greek and German as languages and cultures so that our understanding of the world, while limited by our tradition and by our factual circumstance in history, nevertheless is aided by the proper interpretation of Greek and German language traditions. But I am suggesting that there is a brute contingency to all origins as such, and so the engendering of every tradition is absolutely arbitrary, including the Yahwistic, Shakespearean, and Freudian traditions of seeing the nature and destiny of human beings. And I do not wish to engage "notions of chance, discontinuity and materiality" at the origins of historical ideas, as Foucault does, because I think that Foucault's mode and means of engagement are unknowingly metaphoric. A transference or metaphor takes place when we read J, or Shakespeare, or Freud, just as similar transferences took place when our ancestors read these writers. These transferences, on our part, echo or repeat earlier transferences, and what is transferred is our love for authority, our desire to be augmented by the authority we have invested in the Yahwist, Shakespeare, or Freud. Freud himself, very late in his work, described this investment as the assimilation of the superego to the id, saying that "some of the cultural acquisitions have undoubtedly left a deposit behind in the id; much of what is contributed by the superego will awaken an echo in the id." It is in this context that Freud quotes from the first part of Goethe's *Faust*: "What you have inherited from your fathers, strive to make it your own."

What are the critical consequences of such a notion of facticity? How can it be distinguished from the mere truism that the Yahwist ultimately influences our ideas of God, while Shakespeare shapes our sense of human personality and how it can be represented and Freud informs our prevalent map of the mind? And even if it is not just this truism, of what use is this notion? Does it have pragmatic consequences? Is it a difference that makes a difference, or much difference anyway? I am nothing but a critical pragmatist, and so I advance a working notion of facticity in order to account for a surprise in my own experience as a reader. I have read the Hebrew Bible since my childhood, but only in later years with some sense of modern scholarship, including its intricate, suggestive but necessarily speculative divisions between the likely (if hypothetical) strands that redactors combined into the narratives of Genesis,

Exodus, Numbers. A developing sense that there are incidents, passages, sequences in those stories that are at variance with the prevailing tonality set by the redactors hardly could be avoided by any incessant reader of the Hebrew Bible. Such a sense nevertheless tends to be repressed, which is less a judgment upon even the most skilled and sensitive readers than it is a tribute to the revisionary powers of the normative redactors. As an instance, I remember giving a public lecture on Gnosticism some years ago, during which I made reference to the delight many Gnostics took in the startling episode of Yahweh's attempt to murder Moses. After the lecture, I received several notes asking me to cite the passage, notes sent by authentic and advanced readers. They certainly had read that weird passage in Exodus, but they had gone right past it, defending against the inexplicable by evading it, probably unconsciously.

It is when the odder or more original passages all turn out to be by the J writer that one realizes the anomaly that this inaugural author or "Hebrew Homer" constitutes in regard to the very tradition founded upon him. I say "all" because the story of the *Akedah*, of Abraham being ordered by God to sacrifice Isaac, does not show any stylistic traces of J but is from a literary perspective clearly bowdlerized from J by the Elohistic author or school. Very little of high literary quality in Genesis, Exodus, and Numbers is by any author except J, the largest single exception being the Priestly account of the Creation that begins Genesis. What are we to make of texts that founded themselves upon a great original but which sought to absorb him into a final Scripture very different from his spirit and his procedures? That so much of J remains, and includes so much that is idiosyncratic, would indicate an authority too great to be totally voided by exclusionary rather than revisionary techniques. But what happens then to our ability to read what we can continue to recognize as J?

I recur to my own experience of reading J, first in the context of the redactors, and more recently in his own full strength, which resisted and resists all revisionism. J's redactors, particularly the Priestly authors, would never have asserted that their composite texts represented a fulfillment of J's texts, but rather that they had carried their precursor's work closer to the truth. By the time of the Return, the normative scribes who followed Ezra presumably would have said that all revisions of received material were restorations of the veritable Mosaic text. Certainly from the Return until now the central tradition of Judaism has reinforced this myth of an originary authorship, while continuing to draw upon the ultimate authority of the uncanny J, who may have written three thousand years ago. No Western facticity has been so enduring, or so productive of further strong facticities. Shakespeare swallowed up Marlowe, but we cannot say that he swallowed up the English Bible, or that Freud subsequently quite subsumed Shakespeare, or the Bible. You do not make the Bible, or Shakespeare, into your own fiction, as Lacan made Freud into his (with success rather more indifferent than many believe).

To shape by molding, to make a fiction, is to fashion Adam out of the *adamah,* out of the red clay. Adam is not faked; he is fictitious and not factitious. Yet J's uncanny trope of this fashioning has become another facticity for us. True reading would recover the trope, and yet can any of us avoid literalizing it?

> When there was as yet no shrub of the field upon earth, and as yet no grasses of the field had sprouted, because Yahweh had not sent rain upon the earth, and there was no man to till the soil, but a flow welled up from the ground and watered the whole surface of the earth, then Yahweh molded Adam from the earth's dust (*adamah*), and blew into the nostrils the breath of life, and Adam became a living being.

So far as we know, this is how J got started, by this beginning, which would save all things if its life as trope could dwell among us. J, as I read him, is the most ironic of writers, with a unique irony, resulting always from unresolved clashes of totally incommensurate realities. What are the ironies that we literalize here? Or is it that irony, in J, is our grudging sense of his still unassimilable originality? Contrast his molding of Adam with what he could have found in precursors—whom, however, he rejected as precursors, setting his prose against their mythological verse. But beyond contrast is his choice of starting with the hard Judean spring. No shrub, no grass, but there is that flow welling up from the ground, watering the earth's dust, a welling up that presumably is at Yahweh's will, or should we say *is* Yahweh's will. That welling up is the prelude to Adam, and J's oddly characteristic pun or assonance, his false etymology of Adam from *adamah*, wittily plays for its coherence upon the impishness of the childlike Yahweh. Given some wet clay, he fashions an image, but the model alone would have been a fake, an idol, and not a fiction, except for the spirit blown into our nostrils. Adam is a fake until Yahweh's own breath makes Adam a living being. How many ironies are we to read in this vitalizing fiction?

How else might J have begun? There is the cosmological harvest of Genesis 1, rendered by the P writer many hundreds of years later and altogether antithetical to J in tone and in vision. The God of the Priestly writer is already almost the God of *Paradise Lost*, but J's Yahweh is no schoolmaster of souls. J's Yahweh begins by exercising his own freedom, and the stance of his freedom is conveyed by his choice of the *adamah* as his medium. For what was Adam, what were we, when the image was still unbreathed, when the wet clay still did not have the breath of Yahweh living in it? The first violator of the Second Commandment was Yahweh himself, so that the Commandment says: "Do not presume to be too much like me." But this is inevitably ironic, since Yahweh molded Adam in his own image, a molding which says implicitly: "Be like me" and then adds: "Breathe with my breath." Yahweh himself wanders here between truth and meaning.

Poetry and belief, as I understand them, are antithetical modes of knowledge, but they share the peculiarity of taking place *between* truth and meaning, while being somewhat alienated both from truth and from meaning. Meaning gets started only by or from an excess, an overflow or emanation, that we call originality. Without that excess even poetry, let alone belief, is merely a mode of repetition, no matter in how much finer a tone. So is prophecy, whatever we take prophecy to be.

The Hebrew word *nabi* seems to have meant "proclaimer," so that I suppose we ought to speak of "the proclaimers" rather than "the prophets," but no one among us will choose to do so, since we are deeply invested in the overtones of "the prophets" and "prophecy." We call them "prophets" because the Septuagint translated *nabi* by the Greek word *prophetes,* which means "interpreter." I think that "interpreter" is better than "proclaimer" but we are stuck with the word "prophet," despite its partly irrelevant meaning of foretelling, of predicting an unalterable future. If we go on so, then the result will be so, as Blake said. An interpreter ought to be a seer and not an arbitrary dictator.

Jeremiah indubitably was a seer, but he had something of an arbitrary dictator in him also. He was a great poet but a very unpleasant personality, and I have disliked both him and his book ever since I was a child. Yet in one crucial sense, originality, he is the nearest match to J in the Hebrew Bible, and he is also the crucial link between J and the Book of Job, which Baruch's book of Jeremiah strongly influenced. That redacted book is anything but a literary unity. Its first twenty-five chapters are an anthology of Jeremiah's poetic oracles, presumably gathered by Baruch, his long-suffering scribe, while in Egyptian exile in about 580 B.C.E. Then come two sequences of chapters (26–29, 36–44) written by Baruch, and all the rest seems to be the work of the Deuteronomistic editor or author. The opening six chapters take place about 625 B.C.E., the start of Jeremiah's dreadful career, while 7–25 seem to take us from about 609 to 598 B.C.E.

We know that Jeremiah came of a family very highly connected with political and religious authority in the reign of Josiah the King, but I suggest that we ought to be more interested in Jeremiah's extraordinary psyche than in his politico-spiritual orientation—though doubtless the two matters were closely related. Jeremiah only rarely had visions; perhaps his intimacy with Yahweh was too close for him to need to see. He says: "The God-Word was to me," meaning evidently that his prophecies or poetic interpretations came to him when he was possessed by Yahweh, as in the trance of 4:19–21.

> Oh, my suffering, my suffering!
> How I writhe!
> Oh, the walls of my heart!
> My heart moans within me,
> I cannot be silent;
> For I hear the blare of horns,
> Alarms of war.
> Disaster overtakes disaster,
> For all the land has been ravaged.
> Suddenly my tents have been ravaged.
> In a moment, my tent cloths.
> How long must I see standards
> And hear the blare of horns?

What is translated here as "my suffering" in the Jewish Publication Society version is literally "my entrails" and "For I hear the blare of horns" seems to mean literally "you, my being, hear." That separation from his own being, whether in or out of trance, is characteristic of Jeremiah, and so is that pain in the entrails. John Bright, in the Anchor Bible, has the prophetic bowels writhing, but renders Jeremiah's estranged sense of inner being as the somewhat lackluster "O my soul." Estrangement from self and from others, including many of one's initial supporters, is a particular mark of Jeremiah, but then, had I been his contemporary, I too would have been estranged from him. He was a defeatist, something of a Quisling, a disturbed personality (which is a grand litotes when applied to him), and something of a sadomasochist, particularly where the destruction of Jerusalem was concerned. Though in his initial prophetic call Jeremiah represents himself as a Mosaic figure, and so as an intercessor and mediator, he tells us several times that Yahweh forbade him to intercede, and he believes that the fall of Jerusalem could not have been prevented by any mediator. Babylon took Jerusalem in 597 B.C.E., the city rebelled in 586 and was destroyed, and its upper social class was carried off into exile. Against that terrifying background, Jeremiah takes an unprecedented rhetorical stance, which we can also call psychosexual and cosmological, since rhetoric, psychology, and cosmology are as much one entity for Jeremiah as they were for Heraclitus and Empedocles.

Starting with Chapter 2, Jeremiah's oracles place a heavy emphasis upon the trope of Jerusalem as Yahweh's unfaithful bride, his first wife as it were, to be replaced by the more reliable Jeremiah as second bride. I want to examine this trope more fully in a moment, but only after looking at the most extravagant and memorable passage in this extravagant and memorable interpreter of Yahweh, from the seventh verse of Chapter 20 onward. Here the Hebrew needs to be read very slowly and thoroughly, because Jeremiah accuses Yahweh of sexual violence towards him, an accusation too serious and too original to be set aside as easily as many might wish. Bright renders verse 7 as:

You seduced me, Yahweh, and I let you;
You seized and overcame me.
I've become a daylong joke,
They all make fun of me.

The King James Version, far better as writing, is more ambiguous:

O LORD, thou hast deceived me, and I was deceived: thou art stronger than I, and hast prevailed: I am in derision daily, everyone mocketh me.

The JPS version, less ambiguous in one way, detours in another:

You enticed me, O LORD, and I was enticed;
I have become a constant laughingstock,
Everyone jeers at me.

I think that this is one of the most crucial verses in Jeremiah. W. Rudolph in *Jeremia* (1947) and A. J. Heschel in *The Prophets* (1962) are my precursors here, as is Bright in his somewhat circumspect Anchor commentary. The crucial verbs are *patah* and *chasack*. In Exodus 22:16 *patah* refers to seducing "a maid that is not betrothed" before or without marriage. In Deuteronomy 22:15 *chasack* refers to sexual violence, and elsewhere to adulterous rape. I therefore would render Jeremiah 20:7 as:

Yahweh, you seduced me unlawfully, and I consented to being seduced; you raped me, and you were too strong for my resistance to prevail. All day long I have become an object of derision; everyone mocks me.

This is so extraordinary a trope, and so amazing a blasphemy, that I wonder always why there is not more than perfunctory commentary upon it. As a rhetoric of shock, it matches J's story of Yahweh's motiveless attempt to murder Moses (Exodus 4: 24–25). But J's tone, there as elsewhere, is uncanny, as we have heard. Jeremiah's rhetorical stance has only the shock of originality in common with J's stance. The wrath and pain with which Yahweh speaks, through Jeremiah or else confronting the prophet, is unlike anything in J's Yahweh. *Can* we envision J's Yahweh as being in extreme anguish? Jeremiah's Yahweh protests his despair, his sense of being forsaken and forgotten by his city and his people. It cannot be accidental that Jeremiah places a unique emphasis upon Yahweh's fury and destructiveness, since the antithetical strains of despairing forsakenness and murderous rage mark the poles of the prophet's own personal collapse. Unmarried except to Yahweh, Jeremiah chants of having been overdetermined since before he was created in the womb, consecrated Yahweh's interpreter before birth. The astonishing pathos of Jeremiah's initial protest, that he does not know how to speak because he is still a boy, is dismissed by Yahweh, as though Jeremiah did not need a childhood. Everything that marks this most original of proclaimers—self-division, the augmenting desire for the day of disaster, the guilt of treachery to the principle of his people's independence—is consonant with both his self-presentation and the partisan portraits that Baruch and presumably others give of him.

The hypersensitivity of a *nabi* derided under the name of his constant prophecy (Terror-All-Around) combines with these attributes not to explain, but to render yet more enigmatic his psychosexual blasphemy against Yahweh. We can assume that the political meaning of his scandalous trope was clear enough to his contemporaries. Betrothed to Yahweh in order to replace the harlot Jerusalem, Jeremiah protests the lust of Yahweh, the drive of the rapacious bridegroom who could not wait for the wedding. The daring of this similitude carries

Jeremiah's defiance of the public opinion that nevertheless drives him toward breakdown. Unlike Isaiah, who responds so eagerly to the call, Jeremiah sees himself as overborne from the start. The same pattern informs both, being consecrated in the womb and being the victim of Yahweh's premarital lust. This proclaimer or interpreter wishes his contemporaries and posterity to see his entire career as humanly unwilled. That rhetorical stance accounts for Jeremiah's singular and prevalent use of a dualistic trope of fire, outward and inward, and for his inauguration of a greater dualism, which will become both the normative Jewish and the Freudian dualism, of inwardness against outwardness—a vision unknown to that greatest and most ironic of monists, the J writer.

Heschel distinguishes between the usage of fire in Jeremiah's language as a synecdoche for destruction and for anger. These seem to me both tropes of outwardness: "I will punish you according to your deeds," declares Yahweh; "It shall consume all that is around it" (21:14). Very different are the images of an inward fire, as in the direct aftermath of the prophet's accusation of rape against Yahweh (20:8–16, JPS version):

> For every time I speak, I must cry out,
> Must shout, "Lawlessness and rapine!"
> For the word of the Lord causes me
> Constant disgrace and contempt.
> I thought, "I will not mention Him,
> No more will I speak in His name"—
> But His word was like a raging fire in my heart
> Shut up in my bones;
> I could not hold it in, I was helpless.

Anger and destructiveness, even if Yahweh's, belong to outwardness, and for Jeremiah everything outward is unjust. The Yahweh-Word is an inward fire, however raging, as are the Yahweh-Act and the Yahweh-Thing, since word, act, and thing

are blent in the Hebrew for "word." The inward fire is at one
with prophetic election from before birth, and at one also with
the betrothal to Yahweh, though not with his impatient lust,
which belongs to outwardness. A dualism that is with us still,
of Freud's "frontier concepts" (the bodily ego, the drive, the
nonrepressive defenses of introjection and projection)—not a
dualism of body and soul, or body and mind—is inaugurated
in Jeremiah's magnificent breakthrough, his proclamation of a
new and redeemed relationship of Israel to Yahweh. It is vital
to note that Jeremiah does not proclaim a new Law, or a growing inner self, or a more inward Law. What he interprets instead
is a new opposition between inwardness and outwardness. I
resort to the King James Version of 31:33 here because its elo-
quence alone matches the Hebrew:

> But this shall be the covenant that I will make with the house of
> Israel: After those days, saith the Lord, I will put my law in
> their inward parts, and write it in their hearts: and I will be
> their God, and they shall be my people.

"Inward parts" in the Hebrew might better be translated
"innermost being" or most simply "within them." What matters is Jeremiah's emphasis, here and elsewhere, on the injustice of outwardness and the potential redemptiveness of our
inwardness. That returns us to what has been most consistent
in this wild self-proclaimer, to his extraordinary equation of
sexual passivity, prophetic election, and the worldy virtue of
defeat. Jeremiah himself is as endless to meditation as his true
son, Nietzsche, but I want to conclude with him by turning
our consideration not to this fierce monument of pathos but to
his Yahweh. We have seen that the Yahwist's Yahweh is enormously different from the Yahweh of normative tradition,
Jewish or Christian. How much of the outwardness of the normative Yahweh did Jeremiah invent, not only for himself but

for us as well? Martin Buber, who found himself in Jeremiah, sees precisely what this pathos-laden interpreter proclaimed, a more mysterious Yahweh, getting still more incomprehensible as catastrophes grind onward: "His growing incomprehensibility is mitigated and even compensated by His becoming the God of the sufferers and by suffering becoming a door of approach to Him, as is already clear for the life of Jeremiah where the way of martyrdom leads to an ever purer and deeper fellowship with Yahweh." Some Christians will hear the inception of the Yahweh of Jesus in this; I hear the Yahweh of Job. What I do not hear is the—as it were—original Yahweh of the Yahwist, for J's God was not the God of the sufferers.

The poet of Job emulates a strong precursor, the astonishing prophet Jeremiah. Though the Book of Job is less shocking, rhetorically and dialectically, than Jeremiah's book, it remains profoundly troubling. Like *King Lear*, which is manifestly influenced by it, the Book of Job touches the limits of literature, and perhaps transcends them. Lear desperately prays for patience, lest he go mad, and even declares: "No, I will be the pattern of all patience, / I will say nothing," as though he would be a second Job. In the play's greatest scene (IV.vi), perhaps the finest in Shakespeare or in literature, Lear advises Gloucester to join him in the Jobean fortitude:

> If thou wilt weep my fortunes, take my eyes.
> I know thee well enough, thy name is Gloucester.
> Thou must be patient; we came crying hither.
> Thou know'st, the first time that we smell the air
> We wawl and cry . . .

Patient Job is actually about as patient as Lear is. Ha-satan, the adversary, is provocative enough, but Job's comforters are worse. William Blake bitterly wrote that "in the Book of Job, Milton's Messiah is call'd Satan," and clearly Job's abominable friends are what *The Marriage of Heaven and Hell* calls "Angels," or pious timeservers, fit to become minor officials of Kafka's court or Kafka's castle. Despite pious tamperings, such as the absurd epilogue, the Book of Job is not the work of a trimmer or of a self-deceived saint. Its best expositors remain two fierce Protestants, John Calvin and Søren Kierkegaard.

I take from Calvin his accurate sense that Job does not condemn God, does not accuse him of being "a tyrant or a harebrain." From Kierkegaard, I take his realization that it is not the Behemoth or the Leviathan that causes Job to sink down when God comes at last to confront the sufferer and speaks out of the whirlwind to him. Martin Buber shrewdly notes that "Job cannot forgo either his own truth or God." Protesting the incommensurable, suffering far in excess of sin, Job is answered by a God who speaks only in terms of the incommensurable. The poet of Job returns more to Jeremiah than to the J writer, whose Yahweh is uncanny, but in a different way than the Yahweh of Jeremiah. We are made in Yahweh's image and are asked to be like him, but we are not to presume to be too much like him. He can be argued with, as when Abraham argues him partway down, on the road to Sodom, but he also is subject to peculiar vagaries, as when he tries to murder poor Moses at the outset of the prophet's reluctant mission, or when he alternately entices and warns the people on Sinai. His vagaries are greatest when he rapes Jeremiah. I take it that Job recognizes the reality of Yahweh's extraordinary personality after the voice out of the whirlwind has completed its message, a recognition that is the resolution of the book.

It seems clear to me that the Book of Job is not a theodicy, a justification of the ways of God to man, as Milton defines the genre in his sublime theodicy *Paradise Lost*. The voice out of the whirlwind does not seek to justify. Rather, with an ultimate exuberance, it bombards Job with a great series of rhetorical questions, which attain their summit in the vision of the Leviathan (41:1–7, King James Version):

> Canst thou draw out leviathan with an hook? or his tongue with a cord which thou lettest down?
> Canst thou put an hook into his nose? or bore his jaw through with a thorn?
> Will he make many supplications unto thee? will he speak soft words unto thee?
> Will he make a covenant with thee? wilt thou take him for a servant for ever?
> Wilt thou play with him as with a bird? or wilt thou bind him for thy maidens?
> Shall the companions make a banquet of him? shall they part him among the merchants?
> Canst thou fill his skin with barbed irons? or his head with fish spears?

Ahab's answer in *Moby-Dick* was a fierce affirmative, until his life ended with his outcry: "*Thus,* I give up the spear!" as he rammed his harpoon vainly into the White Whale's sanctified flesh. Job is no Ahab, nor an apocalyptic seer. But it is difficult not to prefer Ahab to Job, when God taunts us with such vicious irony: "Will he make a covenant with thee?" In Kabbalistic prophecy, the companions do make a banquet of the Leviathan when the Messiah comes, but Job is no Kabbalist. The Book of Job is the strong, implicit opponent of that belated doctrine, Gnosticism, and nothing could be further from Job than the Lurianic doctrine of the breaking of the primal vessels of Creation.

Confronted by the Leviathan, Job declares that he had lacked knowledge: "therefore have I uttered that I understood not; things too wonderful for me, which I knew not." The Hebrew text does not say "things too wonderful for me" but "things beyond me." Confronting the sublimity of Yahweh, Job understands his own tradition, which is that the sage must rise to the agon, as Abraham and Jacob did, and so behave pragmatically as if he were everything in himself, while knowing always that, in relation to Yahweh, he is nothing in himself. But I prefer the answering irony of John Calvin: "God would have to create new worlds, if He wished to satisfy us"; or the more complex irony of Kierkegaard: "Fix your eyes upon Job; even though he terrifies you, it is not this he wishes, if you yourself do not wish it." We cannot be satisfied, because Yahweh will create no more new worlds, and we need to be terrified by Job, even if he does not will to terrify us. The limits of desire are also the limits of literature. Kierkegaard is singularly perceptive; it is not the Creation but the Creator who overwhelms Job. Our desires for the good are incommensurate not with the good but with the Creator of good. Shelley, in the accents of Gnosticism, declared that good and the means of good were irreconcilable. Job, in the accents of Jeremiah, accepted his election of adversity, of having been chosen by Yahweh, God of the sufferers.

After three J writers, as it were—the great original J, Jeremiah, and the author of Job—I conclude with a brief coda on a fourth J writer, the author of the humorous and belated Book of Jonah. This curious little book probably came out of the fourth century B.C.E. and has nothing in common with the books of the minor prophets, among which the canon placed it. Jonah refuses initially to accept his election of adversity and flees to Joppa to take ship for Tarshish rather than go up to Nineveh in order to prophesy against it, as commanded by Yahweh. Poor Jonah takes flight precisely because he declines to be the Jeremiah of Nineveh; presumably he thinks he flees the Yahweh of Jeremiah and Job, the God of the sufferers.

After his deliverance from the belly of the great fish, he obeys orders the second time, but to his shock and dismay Nineveh takes the warning, repents, and is saved, which leaves an exceedingly displeased and very angry Jonah.

Jonah seems to me a deliberate parody of Jeremiah; for Nineveh, read Jerusalem, and for Jonah, read the wrathful and suffering Jeremiah himself. The author of Jonah, doubtless using a traditional story, goes back to the benignly uncanny Yahweh of J, a Yahweh with considerable irony and a strong sense of humor. William Tyndale, who set the stance and style still present in the King James Version of the Pentateuch, also translated Jonah, and his accent lingers in the accurately conveyed humor of the original: "Doest thou well to be angry?" Yahweh says to this disappointed parody of Jeremiah, who regrets the lack of destruction, is sheltered from the sun by a gourd, and despairs again when the gourd is withered (4:7–11):

> But God prepared a worm when the morning rose the next day, and it smote the gourd that it withered.
>
> And it came to pass, when the sun did arise, that God prepared a vehement east wind; and the sun beat upon the head of Jonah, that he fainted, and wished in himself to die, and said, It is better for me to die than to live.
>
> And God said to Jonah, Doest thou well to be angry for the gourd? And he said, I do well to be angry, even unto death.
>
> Then said the LORD, Thou hast had pity on the gourd, for the which thou hast not laboured, neither madest it grow; which came up in a night, and perished in a night:
>
> And should not I spare Nineveh, that great city, wherein are more than sixscore thousand persons that cannot discern between their right hand and their left hand; and also much cattle?

The repentant Gentiles of Nineveh do not know their right hand from their left, and cattle ("beasts" in the original) are no more responsible for acts or morals than babies are. We hear J's Yahweh again, incommensurate but shrewdly kind, uncanny yet canny, when he ironically reproves this would-be Jeremiah. How sensible the normative rabbis were in prescribing that we read the Book of Jonah on the afternoon of the Day of Atonement, when we atone for all sins against Yahweh but none against other men and women, a distinction after all more in J's spirit than in Jeremiah's.

II

FROM
HOMER
TO DANTE

FREQUENTLY we forget one reason why the Hebrew Bible is so difficult for us: our only way of thinking comes to us from the ancient Greeks, and not from the Hebrews. No scholar has been able to work through a persuasive comparison of Greek thinking and Hebrew psychologizing, if only because the two modes themselves seem irreconcilable. Attempts to explain this opposition on a linguistic basis have failed, as reductiveness must fail when two such antithetical visions of life are contrasted. Nietzsche remains the best guide I know to the clash of Greek and Hebrew cultures. In *Also Sprach Zarathustra,* he ascribed Greek greatness to the maxim "You shall always be the first and excel all others: your jealous soul shall love no one, unless it be the friend." That certainly describes Achilles in the *Iliad.* Against this Nietzsche sets the maxim that he says the Hebrews hung up as a tablet of overcoming: "To honor father and mother and to follow their will to the root of one's soul." I take it that Nietzsche intended this to describe the Jesus of the Gospels, the son of Yahweh and of the Virgin Mary. I am going to contrast the gods of Homer with the Yahweh of J, but rather than contrast Achilles with Jesus, I will be more timid than Nietzsche and will compare the hero of the *Iliad* with the David of 2 Samuel, written by a great contemporary of the J writer, and also with J's Joseph, since I surmise that J's Joseph is a portrait of the historical David composed in friendly competition with the representation of David in 2 Samuel. Nietzsche's emphasis upon the Greek agonistic spirit presumably derived from his colleague Jakob Burckhardt's insight, but Nietzsche characteristically drove his thought harder than the subtly evasive Burckhardt chose to do. In "Homer's Contest," a fragment from 1872, Nietzsche addresses the issue of Greek agon directly:

The greater and more sublime a Greek is, the brighter the flame of ambition that flares out of him, consuming everybody who runs on the same course. Aristotle once made a list of such hostile contests in the grand manner; the most striking of the examples is that even a dead man can still spur a live one to consuming jealousy. That is how Aristotle describes the relationship of Xenophanes of Calophon to Homer. We do not understand the full strength of Xenophanes' attack on the national hero of poetry, unless—as again later with Plato—we see that at its root lay an overwhelming craving to assume the place of the overthrown poet and to inherit his fame. Every great Hellene hands on the torch of the contest; every great virtue kindles a new greatness . . . (trans. Walter Kaufmann)

Let us note Nietzsche's strong sense of the hostility of the contest, and the role played by jealousy or creative envy. Three years later, in the first half of the fragments for the work "We Philologists," Nietzsche returned to the dangers of agon:

The agonistic element is also the danger in every development; it overstimulates the creative impulse . . .

The greatest fact remains always the precociously panhellenic HOMER. All good things derive from him; yet at the same time he remained the mightiest obstacle of all. He made everyone else superficial, and this is why the really serious spirits struggled against him. But to no avail. Homer always won.

The destructive element in great spiritual forces is also visible here. But what a difference between Homer and the Bible as such a force! (trans. William Arrowsmith)

That difference, at this point, is decided by Nietzsche in Homer's favor. Simone Weil, not a very Nietzschean thinker, read a very different *Iliad* than Nietzsche read, and preferred that *Iliad* to the Hebrew Bible, while finding in the Gospels "the last marvelous expression of the Greek genius, as the *Iliad* is the first." This astonishing judgment, which ends up by

Christianizing the *Iliad*, was founded upon Weil's strong misreading of the *Iliad* as "the poem of force," as when she observed: "Its bitterness is the only justifiable bitterness, for it springs from the subjections of the human spirit to force, that is, in the last analysis, to matter." I am not a classical scholar, but I have never encountered a representation of "the human spirit" in the *Iliad*. "The human spirit," in Weil's sense, ultimately refers back to the distinctive conceptual image of the *ruach-adonai*, the spirit or breath of the Lord, breathed into the nostrils of the clay figure of Adam by J's Yahweh. In Homer's terms, Weil should have ascribed the justifiable bitterness of Achilles and Hector to the subjections of the human force to the gods' force and to fate's force. The *Iliad* does not see men as spirits imprisoned by matter; Homer is not Saint Paul. In the *Iliad*, men are forces that live, perceive, and feel, but the vitality, the perceptions, and the emotions are not integrated. I am following Bruno Snell's portrait of "Homer's view of man," in which Achilles, Hector, and the other warriors "consider themselves a battleground of arbitrary forces and uncanny powers." Snell seems to me still the most illuminating critic I have read on ancient Greek literature, and particularly on the *Iliad*, even more so when grouped with his contemporaries E. R. Dodds and Hermann Fränkel. A deep immersion in current Homeric scholarship has shown me that it mostly evades or even dismisses Snell, Dodds, and Fränkel, probably because they indeed make Homer much more difficult to interpret than any other mode of reading has done. I cite Martin Mueller as not untypical of this trend:

> The Vergilian prism has been no less dominant in the twentieth-century criticism of Homer. If there is a distinguishing feature of twentieth-century criticism, it lies perhaps in the innocent arrogance with which it has claimed a superior understanding on the basis of radically new insights into the nature of

Homer's art or his vision of man. The oral critics in particular have been guilty of a failure to see that their ideological prejudices have a very long history indeed. A somewhat similar charge can be laid against "Homeric anthropologists" like Hermann Fränkel, Bruno Snell, E. R. Dodds, and more recently A. W. H. Adkins. In the works of these scholars, however illuminating it has been on many aspects of the Homeric poems, a Hegelian vision of the unfolding of the human spirit has combined with the scholar's territorial instinct to dwell on the distinctness of his subject and sharply mark off its boundaries. The *homo Homericus* "reconstructed" by their labours is little more than a more scholarly version of the Homeric naive. Whether Parry and Snell are "closer" to the *Iliad* than Chapman or Pope is by no means an idle question. I do not mean to suggest that to study the life of the *Iliad* is to sort through the junkheap of discarded interpretations: on the contrary, the life has a shape and direction that must guide our own understanding. But criticism is not a progressive art.

"Homeric anthropologists" is not a bad phrase for Homer's best critics, just as one hopes that "Yahwistic anthropologists" will arise among the literary students of J. George Chapman and Alexander Pope, as strong poets, shared in one aspect of the *Iliad* that Bruno Snell did not touch, but they do not change my reading of the strongest Western poem as radically as Snell continues to do every time that I reread him. As for Hegel, I do not recall his being mentioned in Snell's masterwork, *The Discovery of the Mind,* and he seems to me far less a presence there than Freud is in Dodds's *The Greeks and the Irrational,* or than Plato is in Fränkel's *Early Greek Poetry and Philosophy.* Snell on Homer is uncannily Homeric, in one sense, just as Milman Parry is in quite another. There is a curious fear among relatively recent Homeric scholars that Snell somehow weakens Homer, or renders the *Iliad* naive, but that is a weak misreading of Snell and his school.

Snell's central insight is that the early Greeks, both in language and in visualization, did not apprehend the human body as a unity, or, as Freud would say, they did not know that the ego is always a bodily ego. They knew the sum total of their limbs, but what we call "body" is a later interpretation of what was initially understood as legs, knees, arms, shoulders. Similarly Homer has no single word to stand for the mind or soul. *Psyche,* for Homer, is not the soul, but is the vitalistic force that keeps us going; it is the organ of life, as it were. Homer uses two other words for what we call the mind, besides *psyche.* These are *thymos,* the organ of emotion or generator of agitation or movement, and *noos,* the organ of perception or cause of images and ideas. *Thymos* persuades you to eat, or hack up your enemy, while *noos* allows you to see and understand.

Fränkel observes usefully that "of all organs of this class the *thymos* is the most comprehensive and at the same time the most spontaneous." Dodds splendidly elucidated its complexities:

> The *thumos* may once have been a primitive "breath-soul" or "life-soul"; but in Homer it is neither the soul nor (as in Plato) a "part of the soul." It may be defined, roughly and generally, as the organ of feeling. But it enjoys an independence which the word "organ" does not suggest to us, influenced as we are by the later concepts of "organism" and "organic unity." A man's *thumos* tells him that he must now eat or drink or slay an enemy, it advises him on his course of action, it puts words into his mouth . . . He can converse with it, or with his "heart" or his "belly," almost as man to man. Sometimes he scolds these detached entities; usually he takes their advice, but he may also reject it and act, as Zeus does on one occasion, "without the consent of his *thumos.*" In the latter case, we should say, like Plato, that the man . . . had controlled *himself.* But for Homeric man the *thumos* tends not to be felt as part of the self: it commonly appears as an independent inner voice. A man may even hear two such voices, as when Odysseus "plans in his *thumos*" to kill the Cyclops forthwith, but a second voice restrains him.

This habit of (as we should say) "objectifying emotional drives," treating them as not-self, must have opened the door wide to the religious idea of psychic intervention, which is often said to operate, not directly on the man himself, but on his *thumos* or on its physical seat, his chest or midriff. We see the connection very clearly in Diomede's remark that Achilles will fight "when the *thumos* in his chest tells him to *and* a god rouses him" (over-determination again).

That "independent inner voice" is neither the Freudian superego nor an auditory hallucination. In Freudian terms, it is closest to a drive, whether Eros or death drive. I suggest that the excitement of reading the *Iliad* is poetically greatly enhanced by the independent if unruly force of the *thymos,* since that force makes Homeric emotions more primal than naive, more imaginative than reductive. Such a force can be measured only in its quantity, rather than its intensity, which must be why Snell tells us that quantity, not intensity, is Homer's standard of judgment. If the intensity of emotion does not matter at all, then there is no psychic motive for any personal decision. A god intervenes, because the Homeric hero cannot see that his own soul or mind is the source of his own powers. One of Snell's sentences that must make our contemporary scholars of Homer very anxious is this, which makes even Achilles something other than a tragic figure, and so perhaps something less: "Mental and spiritual acts are due to the impact of external factors, and man is the open target of a great many forces which impinge on him, and penetrate his very core." This means that all our desires, emotions, and cognitions stem only from the gods. Again, recent scholars tend to find both Homer and Achilles diminished in stature by Snell, and so they deny what seems clearly evident throughout the *Iliad:* character indeed may be fate, yet character, itself a form of knowledge, cannot be distinguished from another character or other knowledge by rival intensities, but only by mere quantity. I remarked in Chapter 1 that J is not anthropomorphic but theomorphic. Homer is anthropomorphic: Achilles is not like Zeus, but Zeus, to a degree, is like Achilles. I would say that in the J writer Yahweh is not like Jacob, but Jacob, to a degree, is like Yahweh. That gives Homer, in my judgment, a poetic advantage over J, but the character of Jacob, or of his son Joseph, or of King David, is clearly distinguished by intensity from the character of Achilles. Yahweh, who does not have human will and feeling, even in J, is also rather more intense in character than is Zeus.

Victory is the highest good in the *Iliad,* and this has over-determined the nature of Western poetry ever since. Even if you are half a god, like Achilles, then finally you cannot attain the highest good. If you are mortal, then you cannot win. Still, you will exemplify the Homeric state of mind, and though that is not a unified state, it is a total one, as Eric Havelock reminds us. In J, the highest good is the Blessing, which exists in a time dimension, *olam,* unknown to Homer, and highly resistant to representation in language. A man moved by his *thymos,* desperate always to win the contest of existence, inevitably defines the poetic hero for us. The subtle and cunning Jacob, J's hero, is both too realistic or canny, and too theomorphic or uncanny, to give us a paradigm for the poetic hero. However, the Homeric gods, despite their felicities and their unamiable failings, remain aesthetic puzzles to us, while the Yahweh of J, thanks to the reductionists and normative revisionists, continues to be an unknown God, despite his impishness and his imaginative vigor.

Achilles is aesthetically enhanced as a representation of human heroism because of the extraordinary, involuntary pathos that ensues from his being a drive or force that lives, perceives, and feels. If he is childlike, perhaps all heroism is childlike, in the context of the Greeks and what we inherit from them, the context of cognition. Each of us, insofar as we remain children of the *Iliad* as our prime educational text, knows herself or himself as a battleground upon which uncanny powers and arbitrary forces meet violently and contend until we end in death. How differently we see ourselves when we alter the prime educational text, and substitute the book of J or 2 Samuel for the *Iliad*. Even as a child, there is little that is childlike about David, and not much more about J's Joseph. Implicitly they possess Yahweh's blessing from the start, which means that each knows that his name will never be scattered. David, and his sly representation in J's Joseph, represent J's vision of a new kind of man, almost a new Adam, the man whom Yahweh has decided to trust, and who will therefore receive Yahweh's covenant-love. The David image, though it will develop a messianic aura later in the Jewish normative tradition, and in Christianity, is in 2 Samuel and in J a vision not of what is to come but of a fully human being who already has exhausted the total range and vitality of human possibility.

If we restore Achilles to the hero of the *Iliad* as Snell, Dobbs, and Fränkel read it, then we will find his aesthetic supremacy absolute, far surpassing even the splendor of 2 Samuel's David, or J's Joseph or even J's Jacob. Dante the pilgrim, and the personages in Chaucer and Shakespeare, will be the first representations of the human that will challenge the immense pathos of Achilles, at once half a child and half a god. J, though uncanny, and somewhat estranged from us by three thousand years of normative revisionism, is by no means wholly other from us. Homer is, and that is his greatest poetic strength. His gods no longer impress us; we wonder at them, or are uneasily amused by them. His heroes are not our heroes, and their radical otherness, particularly that of Achilles, is fated to remain the essence of poetry for us, and the essence also of unbelief.

Achilles' final and most poetic greatness is that he keeps no covenant, except with death.

The Homer of Snell, Dodds, and Fränkel seems to me the Homer that I read, though I doubt I could have read that Homer without them. Virgil, a remarkably accommodating poet, reads to me as an ancestor of our nightmare discontents, our nostalgias, and our fitful hopes for what yet might be. All of the Virgils perhaps fit that ancestry, not only Dante's Virgil and Tennyson's Virgil but our most persuasive contemporary Virgils: that of W. R. Johnson's *Darkness Visible*, with its vision of the terrible reality of Juno's malevolent will; that of Adam Parry's essay on the *Aeneid*'s two voices, Augustan and elegiac; that of K. W. Gransden's Homeric *Aeneid*, with its intertextual subsuming of the *Iliad*; most recently, Wendell Clausen's Alexandrian Virgil, daringly extending the modernist poetics of Callimachus into a precluded mode of poetry, and so achieving the true epic of belatedness.

No one reading the *Aeneid* can endure Juno, who is something more than a nightmare projection of the male fear of female power. Gransden reminds us that there is no villain in the *Iliad*, and that Poseidon's campaign against Odysseus in the *Odyssey* is nothing like the horror of Juno's bitter hatred for Aeneas. Juno, patroness of marriage, is a matron transmogrified into a dangerously convincing monster in the *Aeneid*. I myself, as an amiable disciple of Walter Pater, am enough of an Epicurean to be as frightened by Juno as Virgil was. In his vision, she is fantastic as well as menacing, and certainly she is a very ambiguous achievement in epic representation, being one of the major Western literary instances of what our contemporary feminist critics enjoy calling the projection of male hysteria. I myself would prefer to name Virgil's Juno as the male dread that origin and end will turn out to be one and the same. The only Western image that participates in neither origin nor end is the Hebraic trope of the father, from the Yahwist through Freud; in the *Iliad* the father is not Jacob or Israel, let alone Abraham, but merely Peleus, with whom Achilles has had no relation whatsoever and who is simply a type of ignoble old age wasting toward the wrong kind of death. In the *Aeneid,* the only Western image that is neither origin nor end is reduced to the pathetic figure of Anchises, who has to be carried out of burning Troy upon the shoulders of his priggishly pious son, the heroic but not unambiguous Aeneas.

I am afraid that the dominant image of the mother in the *Aeneid* is not that of Venus, the actual mother, but rather the hardly maternal Juno, rouser of the world below, the Hell of the fury Allecto and the ghastly Dira, manifesting as a gruesome carrion bird. Dante's Virgil has little actually in common with the poet of the *Aeneid,* except that Allecto and the Dira are worthy of Dante's *Inferno,* and so indeed is Juno. There is a dark sense in which Juno is Virgil's pragmatic muse, the drive of his poem. When she vows to give Lavinia a dowry of blood, Trojan and Latin, with Bellona as a bridesmaid, we hear in her Virgil's authentic if repressed aggressivity toward his daunting father, Homer. Inspiring an agonistic intensity in the subtle Epicurean, Virgil, she comes to speak for the poet himself when he confronts the *Iliad* and the *Odyssey:*

> if my powers fall short,
> I need not falter over asking help
> Wherever help may lie. If I can sway
> No heavenly hearts I'll rouse the world below.
>   (trans. Robert Fitzgerald)

Is that not Virgil's peculiar achievement as compared with Homer's, the creation of Juno's world? Juno herself is Virgil's signature, the mark of his principal originality as a poet. She *is* his imagination, insofar as it is his own, and not Homer's. The pathos of her world is that it engulfs not Aeneas and Lavinia but Turnus and Dido, the two most sympathetic and aesthetically gratifying personages in the poem. Turnus, not Aeneas, is the figure worth comparing to Achilles and to David, and to Joseph as David's surrogate in J, just as Juno, rather than Jove, ought to be compared to the *Iliad*'s Zeus and to the J writer's Yahweh. If Juno is the principle of anxiety in the *Aeneid*, Turnus is the object of Virgil's own love, his pride in his own fictive creation. He was not writing the *Turneid*, but we can suspect he would have been happier doing so, and Book 12 is in any case a miniature *Turneid*, even as Book 4 belongs to Dido, and not to Aeneas. All of Book 12 is a self-wounding on Virgil's part, an epiphany of lacerations and self-destroyings. Gransden makes the fine observation that "a view of war emerges which is closer to that of Wilfred Owen than to Homer," and then compares Turnus in the epic's final moments to Marlowe's Faustus in his final scene. I would invoke Hotspur, despite Turnus having no antic wit, because Hotspur and Turnus attract us by their peculiarly violent natures, at once neurotic and appealing.

Turnus dies a terrible death, which in some sense was also the death of Virgil, or at least of Virgil's poetry. Hector dies badly, with great loss of dignity, but compared to Turnus Hector dies with a Hemingwayesque or Spanish grandeur. Achilles remains the hero in killing Hector, but both Turnus and Aeneas have their heroism drained from them, since Turnus truly is slaughtered by Jove, who first imposes his will upon Juno and then becomes quite indistinguishable from her. The Dira sickens the wretched Turnus, numbing him until this giant force does not know anything, even himself. He stands defenseless, unable to speak, trapped grotesquely in a waking nightmare.

Aeneas hurls a spear into a mere object, not a man, and the poem breaks off abruptly, with a gratuitous butchery.

Juno has so contaminated Jove that we are left wondering just what Virgil's vision of the divine possibly can be. One can imagine the reactions of Virgil's precursor, Lucretius, to this not exactly Epicurean vision of the divine reality. If the gods of the *Iliad,* in their better aspect, compensate for minds in which there is no unity and no control, then the gods of the *Aeneid* give nothing and take away nearly everything. Achilles is both a child and a god, but Turnus is childish rather than childlike, and finally he is just one more victim of the madness of war. The poetry of the *Aeneid* takes place well between truth and meaning, resigned to being estranged from both. If there is belief in the *Aeneid,* then it simply vanishes in the second half of the poem. It is not so much estranged from truth and from meaning as it is in deliberate exile of flight from both. Virgil is powerful in his repressions, and even more in his returns of the repressed. J represses nothing; his Abraham, Jacob, and particularly his David surrogate, Joseph, have each a unified consciousness and a directed will. The gods of the *Iliad* are infinitely remote from J's Yahweh, but Juno and Jove in the *Aeneid* look dangerously like the fallen angels or devils in *Paradise Lost*. Homer's final victim may have been Virgil, who was not suited to the field of agon, and there is something unintentionally cruel in the title of Gransden's study, *Virgil's Iliad*. How ironically we would regard the title *Homer's Aeneid*. J and the *Iliad* continue to dispute the palm of representation, until we come to Dante, Virgil's daemonic son.

I will not begin my consideration of Dante by preferring the Crocean Dante of modern Italian criticism to the theological Dante of contemporary American criticism, the Dante of Erich Auerbach, Charles Singleton, and John Freccero. Without

Freccero, I would find it difficult to read Dante, but there seem to me two quite distinct Frecceros. One is the continuator of Auerbach and Singleton, and gives us what I would call the conversion of poetics into Paul and Augustine. The other, whom I follow, takes a Nietzschean, agonistic view of Dante, a view I find also in a critic I greatly prefer to Auerbach, Ernst Robert Curtius. Doubtless poetic form and theological significance are inseparable and pragmatically unified in Dante, but they are not and cannot be one and the same entity. Dante's theology and his politics did fuse, but belief and poetry cannot. I am going to compare Dante the pilgrim and Dante the poet to Achilles, David, and Joseph as representatives of heroism, and I also intend to contrast implicitly Dante's heavenly ladies—Beatrice, Lucia, and the unnamed higher being who bids them to intervene in the poem's action—both to the Homeric gods and to J's Yahweh. But I cannot proceed to these agonistic confrontations until I argue a little, with infinite respect, against Auerbach, Singleton, and Freccero and their rigorous insistence upon functioning wholly within Pauline interpretive categories of the letter and the spirit, categories that I find frequently irrelevant to the crucial figurations of the *Commedia*.

Singleton remarks that "the fiction of the *Divine Comedy* is that it is not a fiction." That joins the issue: that his poem is not a fiction is Dante's agon with all previous fictions. Curtius insists that Dante saw himself as an apocalyptic figure or a prophet, with expectations that the prophecy would be fulfilled in his own lifetime. Presumably this sanctioned Dante's audacity in claiming for his Beatrice a place in the objective process of salvation for all believers, not just for Dante. Like Joachim of Flora, Dante is the author of a personal gnosis. Through Beatrice alone, the race of man excels all that is under the moon, all that is earthly. Lucia, a rather obscure martyr from Syracuse, is exalted by Dante as the particular enemy of all cruelty. She sends Beatrice to Dante, and she herself is sent by an even higher heavenly lady, whom we have no reason to believe is the Virgin Mary. Curtius reminds us how sublimely arbitrary this is. It does not stem from Paul or from Augustine. Manifestly it is an allegory, but if it is an allegory of the theologians and not of the poets, then we do not know who these inventive theologians are.

Singleton apparently followed Dante himself in exalting the allegory of the theologians over the allegory of the poets. In the allegory of the poets, the first or literal sense is a fiction, and the second or allegorical sense is the true one; thus, Orpheus and his music constitute a fiction, but it is true that Orphic wisdom tames cruel hearts. In biblical or theological allegory, the literal sense is true and historical, and the second or allegorical sense is spiritual, being an interpretation of fact and history. Thus the Exodus, when Israel went out of Egypt, is supposedly a historical fact, but spiritually interpreted it is our redemption by Christ. On this distinction between an allegory of the poets that is so palpably weak and an allegory of the theologians at once true and prophetic, it is obvious why Dante made his choice. But it is not quite the same choice when Singleton and the Singletonian side of Freccero try to follow Dante. Singleton sensibly reminds us that "Beatrice is not Christ" although her advent is an analogy to the advent of Christ:

> Thus it is that the figure of a rising sun by which Beatrice comes at last to stand upon the triumphal chariot is the most revealing image which the poet might have found not only to affirm the analogy of her advent to Christ's in the present tense, but to stress, in so doing, the very basis upon which that analogy rests: the advent of light.

Charles Williams, in his study *The Figure of Beatrice,* says that "the entire work of Dante . . . is a description of the great act of knowledge, in which Dante himself is the Knower, and God is the Known, and Beatrice is the Knowing." Can we, with Singleton, accept her as an analogy or, with Williams, as Dante's knowing or gnosis, or is she now the principal embarrassment of Dante's poem? As a fiction she retains her astonishing force, but does not Dante present her as more than a fiction, as a theological or biblical allegory? How are we to recapture Dante's sense of Beatrice if we cannot accept the analogy of her advent to Christ's? Singleton's answer is that Beatrice is the representation of wisdom in a Christian sense, or of the light of grace. That is not poetically persuasive, unless its analogical matrix is light rather than grace. Yet Dante persuades not by his theology but by his uncanny mastery of the trope of light, a mastery in which he surpasses even the blind Milton among the poets. Here is *Paradiso* 30:100–102, in John Sinclair's translation (which I use throughout, with one exception): "There is a light up there which makes the Creator visible to the creature, who finds his peace only in seeing Him."

This, Singleton says, is the light of glory rather than the light of grace, which is Beatrice's, or the natural light, which is Virgil's. Dante's peculiar gift supposedly is to have found perpetually valid analogies for all three lights. Since his poem's fiction of duration is not temporal but final, all three modes of light must be portrayed by him as though they were beyond change. And yet an unchanging fiction cannot give pleasure, as Dante clearly knew. What does he give us that more than compensates for his poem's apparent refusal of temporal anguish?

Auerbach's answer was the trope of *figura*: "*something real and historical* which announces something else that is also real and historical." Cato of Utica in the first canto of *Purgatorio* is a famous Auerbachian example, which I wish to worry a bit, for a moment. How is the historical Cato of Utica the *figura* of Dante's Cato of Purgatory? The historical Cato sought freedom, but he was a pagan, an opponent of Caesar, and a suicide. Auerbach argues that Cato's quest for civic freedom finds its fulfillment in the Christian freedom through purgation that Dante sets him to supervise. Yes, but that quest for freedom was expressed through his suicide, itself an act of his anti-Caesarism and his paganism. And is the historical Virgil truly a *figura* of which Dante's Virgil is the fulfillment?

Is the poet Virgil in any way more reasonable than, say, the poet Horace? Like Lucretius, but less dogmatically, Virgil was an Epicurean. Dante could have relied upon Virgil's Epicurean consciousness of pain, with its deep awareness that the cosmos and the gods were unreasonable, as an intimation that Virgil needed Christianity. Instead, Dante strongly misread Virgil as a believer in a rational cosmos. But Dante, and Auerbach, and Saint Paul, cannot really have it both ways at once. You cannot say that Virgil in Dante's *Comedy* is the historical Virgil, but then again is not. If the historical Virgil or Cato or Moses or Joshua is only a *figura* of the fulfilled truth that Dante's *Comedy,* or the New Testament, reveals, then this fulfillment necessarily is more real, more replete with significance, than the *figura* was or is. As soon as Virgil or Cato, Moses or Joshua, becomes less significant or real than Dante or Jesus or Saint Paul, then the *Aeneid* and the Hebrew Bible also become less significant and less real than the *Comedy* or the New Testament. Indeed, the *Aeneid* and the Hebrew Bible are replaced. Instead of Virgil's *Aeneid,* the nightmare poem dominated by the sinister Juno and her horrible ministers Allecto and the Dira, we get Dante's tamer or castrated *Aeneid,* which dwindles eventually into Matthew Arnold's and T. S. Eliot's banal and priggish *Aeneid.* Instead of the Hebrew Bible of J, Jeremiah, and Job, we get that captive work, the Old or indeed senescent Testament, considerably less vital than the New Testament. The Hebrew Bible becomes the letter, while Saint Paul and Saint John become the spirit.

In merest fact, and so in history, no text can fulfill another, except through some self-serving caricature of the earlier text by the later. To argue otherwise is to indulge in a dangerous idealization of the relationship between literary texts, akin to Singleton's idealization of the allegory of the theologians. Both stances—Auerbach's and Singleton's—refuse the temporal anguish of literary history. We have learned that Freud's later account of repetition compulsion is the final Western *figura*, prophesying our urge to drive beyond the pleasure principle. For us, now, the only text that can fulfill earlier texts, rather than correct or negate them, is what ought to be called the text of death, which is totally opposed to what Dante sought to write.

The earlier Auerbach, seer of Dante as poet of the secular world, seems to me a better guide than the Auerbach who became the prophet of *figura*. Dante's way of representing reality, according to the earlier Auerbach, was to depict not the Homeric "time in which destiny gradually unfolds, but the final time in which it is fulfilled." If time indeed is finality, beyond all unfolding, then reality indeed can be represented in a single act that is both character and fate. Dante's men and women reveal themselves totally in what they say and do, but they do not and cannot change *because* of what Dante has them say or do. Chaucer, though he was more indebted to Dante than he would acknowledge, departed from Dante precisely in this, a departure that constitutes the largest Chaucerian influence upon Shakespeare. The Pardoner listens to himself speaking, is moved by his own sermon and his own tale, and is made more doom-eager through just that listening. This mode of representation expands in Shakespeare to a perfection that no writer since has attained so consistently. Hamlet may be the most bewilderingly metamorphic of Shakespeare's people, but as such he helps establish what becomes the general mode. Nearly everyone of consequence in Shakespeare helps to inaugurate a mimetic mode that has naturalized itself for us, so that it now contains us, as it were; it has become a contingency that we do not recognize as such. Shakespeare's characters (and we ourselves) are strengthened or victimized, reach an apotheosis or are destroyed, by themselves (like ourselves) reacting to what they say and do. It may be more than an irony to observe that we have learned to affect ourselves so strongly, in part, because involuntarily we imitate Shakespeare's characters. We never imitate Dante's creatures because we do not live in finalities; we know that we are not fulfilled.

Freccero, student of Singleton and disciple of Auerbach, happily is prevented from vanishing utterly into their idealizing historicisms by his keen sense of the agonistic basis of Dante's actual poetics, a sense in which Curtius is Freccero's precursor. Freccero's Singletonian emphasis upon a "poetics of conversion" misrepresents, to a surprising degree, his own praxis as a critic of Dante, which is always to locate the strength of what I would call Dante's transumptions or metaleptic reversals of all poetic precursors—Latin, Provençal, and Italian. This returns Freccero, and ourselves, to the earlier Auerbach's emphasis upon Dante's originality in the representation of persons. As seer, Dante identified character with fate, *ethos* with the *daimon,* and what he saw in his contemporaries he transferred to the three final worlds of *Inferno, Purgatorio,* and *Paradiso.* Dante's friends and enemies alike are beheld by us, shown to us without ambivalence or ambiguity, as being consistent with themselves, beyond change, their eternal destinies overdetermined not by God and the angels but by their own fixed characters.

There are perpetual surprises in his *Comedy* for Dante himself, as for us, but there are no accidents. The magnificent Farinata, as sublimely proud as Milton's Satan, stands upright in his tomb, as if of Hell he had a great disdain, and he is heroic, because he is massively consistent with himself: he can be nothing but what he is. But his poetic splendor has little to do with the allegory of the theologians, as that is simply not an available mode for us any longer, despite Auerbach's devotion to *figura*, Singleton's passion for Thomas Aquinas, and Freccero's reliance upon Augustine as the inventor of the novel of the self. Singleton, in rejecting the allegory of the poets, said that it would reduce Dante's Virgil to a mere personification of reason. I would reply that Virgil, an allegory of the poets indeed, should be read not as Reason, the light of nature, but as the trope of that light, reflecting among much else the lusters of the tears of universal nature. When Dante says farewell to Virgil, he takes leave not of Reason but of the pathos of a certain natural light. Dante abandons Virgil not to seek grace but to find his own image of voice. In the oldest and most authentic allegory of the poets, Virgil represents poetic fatherhood, the scene of instruction that Dante must transcend if he is to complete his journey to Beatrice.

Beatrice is the most difficult of all Dante's tropes, because sublimation no longer seems a human possibility. One highly respected feminist critic has characterized Beatrice as a "dumb broad," presumably because she contemplates the One without understanding Him. I venture that Beatrice is now so difficult to apprehend precisely because she participates both in the allegory of the poets and in that of the theologians. Since her advent follows Dante's poetic maturation, or the vanishing of Virgil the precursor, Beatrice is a poetic allegory of the Muse, whose function is to help the poet remember. Remembering is, in poetry, always the major mode of cognition, so Beatrice is Dante's power of invention, the essence of his art. Already the highest of the Muses, Beatrice is also far above them because she has the status of a heretical myth, a saint canonized by Dante, or even an angel created by him. It is now customary to speak of Dante as *the* Catholic poet, even as Milton is called *the* Protestant poet. Perhaps someday Kafka will be named as *the* Jewish writer, though his distance from normative Judaism is infinite. Dante and Milton were not less idiosyncratic, each in his own time, than Kafka is in ours, and the figure of Beatrice would be heresy and not myth if Dante had not been so strong a poet that the Church of later centuries has been happy to claim him. Auerbach knew that Dante was not Tertullian, while Singleton escaped his own temptation of confounding Aquinas with Dante, and Freccero does not confuse Dante and Augustine. Unfortunately, the readers of all three critics sometimes seem to have learned to read Dante precisely as they would read theology. A distorted emphasis upon doctrine is the unhappy result, and soon readers forget the insight of Curtius, which is that Dante's Beatrice is the central figure in a purely personal gnosis. Dante was a ruthless visionary, passionately ambitious and desperately willful, whose poem triumphantly expresses his own unique personality. The *Comedy* is not an allegory of the theologians, but an immense trope of pathos or power, the power of the singular individual who was Dante.

Dante the pilgrim and Virgil the guide are not simply Dante the poet and Virgil the poet, any more than the heavenly lady Beatrice is simply Beatrice, daughter of the Florentine banker Portinari. They are three extraordinary representations, not of any theological code but of an intensely personal myth or story: audacious, ambitious, and avowedly prophetic. Dante has little real interest in being Pauline, Augustinian, or Thomistic; only in being Dante the prophet, who is decidedly *not* Dante the pilgrim, but just as decidedly *is* Dante the poet. I cite Curtius again on Dante as the prophet of a Newer Testament, at once imperial and vengeful, and with virtues that may be Christian only in a particular sense:

Dante's system is built up in the first two cantos of the *Inferno*, it supports the entire *Commedia*. Beatrice can be seen only within it. The Lady Nine has become a cosmic power which emanates from two superior powers. A hierarchy of celestial powers which intervene in the process of history—this concept is manifestly related to Gnosticism: as an intellectual construction, a schema of intellectual contemplation, if perhaps *not* in origin.

Very little American Dante criticism has followed the lead of Curtius, who might have dissuaded some critics from their endless emphasis upon Dante's supposed theological orthodoxy. Curtius did not mean that Dante was a Gnostic, but he did remind us that Dante's Beatrice is at the center of an idiosyncratic gnosis. Critics who read Dante in terms of an Augustinian poetics of conversion are like those who read Milton as Christian doctrine, from C. S. Lewis through many contemporary reductionists of poetry to theology. Dante, like Milton, was essentially a sect of one, not as pilgrim, but as prophetic poet. Milton was Bible-haunted and yet attempted things both in competition with and even beyond the scope of the Bible. The *Comedy*, for all its learning, is not deeply involved in the Bible, and I doubt John Freccero's learned contention "that we are to regard Dante's entire spiritual autobiography as essentially Augustinian in structure." Freccero has enormous authority for me, but Dante's poem, as Curtius saw, is a spiritual testament more in the manner of Joachim of Flora than in that of Augustine. Is the *Comedy* primarily a spiritual autobiography, as Freccero says, or is it a prophecy, as Curtius avers? Spiritual autobiography, whether in Augustine, Rousseau, or Wordsworth, patiently awaits the fullness of time and does not seek an end to history. Prophecy batters at history and has a tendency to turn apocalyptic, to hasten the end. Dante was no more humble or patient by nature than Milton was, and he must have enjoyed his own fierce irony when, in Canto XII of the *Paradiso,* he has Bonaventura, enemy of the Everlasting Gospel of Joachim of Flora, nevertheless praise Joachim as "endowed with a spirit of prophecy."

It is Dante's own ancestor, the Crusader Cacciaguida, who acclaims his descendant as a prophet three cantos later, after greeting the poet as the singular being to whom heaven's gate opened twice. Most crucially, Cacciaguida addresses his great-great-grandson as the reader not of the Bible or Augustine or Virgil but of "the great volume where there is never change of black or white," the book of God's foreknowledge of the truth, a third Testament which is not Joachim of Flora's Everlasting Gospel and therefore is clearly the *Comedy* itself. Seeing that Dante recognizes him and knows his ancestor to be the most joyful of the happy crowd around him, Cacciaguida gives Dante the principle of the poet's prophetic vocation, which establishes the authority of the *Comedy:* "You behold the truth, for the small and great of this life gaze into that mirror, in which, before you think, you behold your thought." I do not think this is an allusion to Psalm 139:2, "You understand my thought from afar," because no distance is involved in Cacciaguida's trope, whether from God or from the self. Dante, through his heroic great-great-grandfather, salutes himself as that unique one, all but messianic, who beheld the truth in his own image before ever he began to think. Not an Augustinian Dante, but a more than Joachim, is addressed here, to be told subsequently "things which shall be incredible to those that witness them," secrets that Dante will only hint at in his poem. Has any poet ever celebrated himself as astonishingly as Dante now is celebrated by his ancestor? "Conscience dark with its own or another's shame will indeed feel thy words to be harsh; but none the less put away every falsehood and make plain all thy visions . . . This cry of thine shall do as does the wind, which strikes most on the highest summits; and that is no small ground of honor."

With a poet so preternaturally strong as Dante, we should look for what is not there, and what is absent in this magnificent accolade is any reference to a biblical trope, whether prophetic, as in Isaiah or Jeremiah, or relating to Christ, in the Gospels or in Paul. Dante's revelation is his own, and will be of himself. There is a blending in Cacciaguida's peroration between Dante the pilgrim and Dante the poet, who thus become exalted in one another. As poetic, indeed as epic hero, Dante himself takes the place of Aeneas, and so ultimately of Achilles, and achieves a status comparable to David, at once true poet and peculiarly favored by God. We are given again the pathos of a great personality, hardly any man's follower, Augustine's or Virgil's, and needing only Beatrice, his own creation, as his guide. The supreme pathos of that personality, poet as well as pilgrim, is most felt in the great and final parting of Beatrice from her poet, in the midst of *Paradiso,* Canto XXXI, at the moment when her place as guide is transferred to the aged Saint Bernard:

Already my glance had taken in the whole general form of Paradise but had not yet dwelt on any part of it, and I turned with new-kindled eagerness to question my Lady of things on which my mind was in suspense. One thing I intended, and another encountered me: I thought to see Beatrice, and I saw an old man, clothed like that glorious company. His eyes and his cheeks were suffused with a gracious gladness, and his aspect was of such kindness as befits a tender father. And "Where is she?" I said in haste; and he replied: "To end thy longing Beatrice sent me from my place; and if thou look up into the third circle from the highest tier thou shalt see her again, in the throne her merits have assigned to her."

Without answering, I lifted up my eyes and saw her where

she made for herself a crown, reflecting from her the eternal beams. From the highest region where it thunders no mortal eye is so far, were it lost in the depth of the sea, as was my sight there from Beatrice; but to me it made no difference, for her image came down to me undimmed by aught between.

"O Lady in whom my hope has its strength and who didst bear for my salvation to leave thy footprints in Hell, of all the things that I have seen I acknowledge the grace and the virtue to be from thy power and from thy goodness. It is thou who hast drawn me from bondage into liberty by all those ways, by every means for it that was in thy power. Preserve in me thy great bounty, so that my spirit, which thou hast made whole, may be loosed from the body well-pleasing to thee." I prayed thus; and she, so far off as she seemed, smiled and looked at me, then turned again to the eternal fount.

There is a frightening strength in this, in its apparent sublimation of a mythmaking drive that here accepts a restraint that is at once rhetorical, psychological, and cosmological. Freud, in his own great summa, "Analysis Terminable and Interminable," lamented his failure to cure those who would not accept the cure: "A man will not be subject to a father-substitute or owe him anything and he therefore refuses to accept his cure from the physician." Dante too would not owe any man anything, not even if the man were Virgil, his poetic father, or Augustine, his conversionary forerunner. The cure was accepted by Dante from his physician, Beatrice, but she was his own creation, the personal myth that centered his poem. In smiling and looking at him as they part, she confirms the cure.

III

SHAKESPEARE

THERE ARE only three significant literary influences upon Shakespeare: Marlowe, Chaucer, and the English Bible. Marlowe was swallowed up by Shakespeare, as a minnow by a whale, though Marlowe had a strong enough aftertaste to compel Shakespeare to some wry innuendos. We can surmise that Marlowe became for Shakespeare a warning: not the way to go. Chaucer suggested to Shakespeare what became his principal resource and at last his greatest originality in the representation of persons. The English Bible had an ambiguous effect upon the writer who has been its only rival in forming the rhetoric and vision of all who came after in the language. Shakespeare's use of the Geneva and Bishops' Bibles, and of the biblical portions of the Book of Common Prayer, is a resort not to belief but to poetry. We have learned much more from Shakespeare than we generally realize. One of many truths he goes on teaching us is that belief is a weak misreading of literature, even as poetry depends upon a strong or creative misreading of prior poetic strength.

Our greatest difficulty in rereading or attending Shakespeare is that we experience no difficulty at all, which is more than a paradox, since we confront a poetic strength that surpasses even the Yahwist, Homer, Dante, and Chaucer. We cannot see the originality of an originality that has become a contingency or facticity for us. I remember observing to a faculty seminar on Shakespeare that not only did our habitual modes for representing persons by language originate with Shakespeare, but also we owed to him most of our supposedly modern ways of representing cognition by writing and reading. One scholar present protested that I was mistaking Shakespeare for God. To say that, after God, Shakespeare has invented most is actually to note that most of what we have naturalized in prior

literary representation stems first from the J writer and his revisionists, and from Homer, but secondarily and yet more
powerfully from Shakespeare.

The most vital single element in Shakespeare brings us back
to Chaucer. The scholarly discussions of Chaucer's influence
upon Shakespeare can be said to have culminated in the late
E. Talbot Donaldson's accomplished *The Swan at the Well:
Shakespeare Reading Chaucer*, with its coda comparing the
Wife of Bath and Falstaff as two great comic vitalists. My own
interest concerns influence of a more repressed sort. Chaucer,
rather than Marlowe or even the English Bible, was Shakespeare's central precursor in having given the dramatist the
crucial hint that led to the greatest of his originalities: the representation of change by showing people pondering their own
speeches and being altered through that consideration. We
find this mode of representation commonplace and even natural, but it does not exist in Homer or in the Bible, in Euripides
or in Dante. One formal aspect of this Shakespearean originality was noted by Hegel in his posthumously published lectures, *The Philosophy of Fine Art:*

> the more Shakespeare on the infinite embrace of his world-
> stage proceeds to develop the extreme limits of evil and folly, to
> that extent . . . he concentrates these characters in their limita-
> tions. While doing so, however, he confers on them intelligence
> and imagination; and, by means of the image in which they, by
> virtue of that intelligence, contemplate themselves objectively
> as a work of art, he makes them free artists of themselves . . .

Hamlet, Edmund, Iago, Falstaff—this very diverse fourfold
are allied only as free artists of themselves, and by virtue of
their own powers they can contemplate themselves objectively
as works of art. Such a contemplation is peculiarly effective
when it activates the most unnerving quality of great art,
which is a capacity for both bringing about and manifesting
human change. What allies certain figures in Chaucer—the

Pardoner and the Wife of Bath in particular—to Shakespeare is just such a self-contemplation and metamorphic reaction. The Pardoner and the Wife of Bath are well along the mimetic path that leads to Edmund and Falstaff. What they say to others, and to themselves, partly reflects what they already are, but also partly begets what they yet will be. Even more subtly, Chaucer intimates ineluctable transformations in the Pardoner and the Wife of Bath through the effect of the language of the tales that they choose to tell. In Homer and the Bible and Dante, we are not shown sea-changes in particular persons brought about by those persons' own language, through the differences that individual diction and tonalities make as speech engenders further speech.

A. D. Nuttall, in his very useful study *A New Mimesis: Shakespeare and the Representation of Reality* (1983), makes an approach to Shakespeare's greatest strength, his cognitive and representational originality:

> In the cultural analysis of ancient texts there is a running presumption that the hope of truth is increasingly confined to the analysis itself and is removed from the material analysed: *their* perceptions are unconsciously conditioned but *we* can identify the conditions. The example of Shakespeare is endlessly rebellious against this arrogant relegation. Even when one works with seemingly modern tools of thought, such as the concepts of cultural history, one finds that Shakespeare is there before one. The inference is obvious: the text refuses to relinquish what I have called "the hope of truth." Its level of *cognitive* activity is so high that later attempts to compass even the latent character of thought-categories find that its most radical moves have been anticipated by the poet. The easiest way—no, the *only* way—to account for this is to say that Shakespeare was looking very hard at the same world (400 years younger, but still the same world) that we are looking at now.

Shakespeare indeed is always there before one; he contains cultural history, Freud, and what you will, and has anticipated every move to come. But I cannot agree with Nuttall that Shakespeare observed our world, unchanged then from now. Rather, I suggest that the difference between the world that Shakespeare saw and ours is to an astonishing degree Shakespeare himself. To define that difference, I take us to the final act of *Hamlet*.

It is a critical commonplace to assert that the Hamlet of Act V is a changed man: mature rather than youthful, certainly quieter if not quietistic; somehow more attuned to divinity. Perhaps the truth is that he is at last himself, no longer afflicted by mourning and melancholia, by murderous jealousy and incessant rage. Certainly he is no longer haunted by his father's ghost. It may be that the desire for revenge is fading in him. In all of Act V he does not speak once of his dead father directly. There is a single reference to "my father's signet" which serves to seal up the doom of those poor schoolfellows, Rosencrantz and Guildenstern, and there is the curious phrasing of "my king" rather than "my father" in the half-hearted rhetorical question the prince addresses to Horatio:

> Does it not, think thee, stand me now upon—
> He that hath kill'd my king and whor'd my mother,
> Popp'd in between th'election and my hopes,
> Thrown out his angle for my proper life
> And with such coz'nage—is't not perfect conscience
> To quit him with this arm?

When Horatio responds that Claudius will hear shortly from England, presumably that Rosencrantz and Guildenstern have been executed, Hamlet rather ambiguously makes what might be read as a final vow of revenge:

> It will be short. The interim is mine.
> And a man's life's no more than to say "one."

However this is to be interpreted, Hamlet forms no plot and is content with a wise passivity, knowing that Claudius must act. Except for the scheme of Claudius and Laertes, we and the prince might be confronted by a kind of endless standoff. What seems clear is that the urgency of the earlier Hamlet has gone. Instead, a mysterious and beautiful disinterestedness dominates this truer Hamlet, who compels universal love precisely because he is beyond it, except for its exemplification by Horatio. What we overhear is an ethos so original that we still cannot assimilate it:

> Sir, in my heart there was a kind of fighting
> That would not let me sleep. Methought I lay
> Worse than the mutines in the bilboes. Rashly—
> And prais'd be rashness for it: let us know
> Our indiscretion sometime serves us well
> When our deep plots do pall; and that should learn us
> There's a divinity that shapes our ends,
> Rough-hew them how we will—

Weakly read, that divinity is Jehovah, but more strongly "ends" here are not our intentions but rather our fates, and the contrast is between a force that can *shape* stone, and our wills that only hew roughly against implacable substance. Nor would a strong reading find Calvin in the echoes of the Gospel of Matthew as Hamlet sets aside his own will: "Thou wouldst not think how ill all's here about my heart." In his heart, there is again a kind of fighting, but the readiness, rather than the ripeness, is now all:

> Not a whit. We defy augury. There is special providence in the fall of a sparrow. If it be now, 'tis not to come; if it be not to come, it will be now; if it be not now, yet it will come. The readiness is all. Since no man, of aught he leaves, knows aught, what is't to leave betimes? Let be.

The apparent nihilism more than negates the text cited from Matthew, yet the epistemological despair presents itself not as despair but as an achieved serenity. Above all else, these are not the accents of an avenger, or even of someone who still mourns, or who continues to suffer the selfish virtues of the natural heart. Not nihilism but authentic disinterestedness, and yet what is that? No Elizabethan lore, no reading in Aristotle, nor even in Montaigne, can help to answer that question. We know the ethos of disinterestedness only because we know Hamlet. Nor can we hope to know Hamlet any better by knowing Freud. The dead father indeed was, during four acts, more powerful than the living one could be, but by Act V the dead father is not even a numinous shadow. He is merely a precursor, the Hamlet the Dane before this one, and this one matters much more. The tragic hero in Shakespeare, at his most universally moving in Hamlet, is a representation so original that conceptually *he contains us,* and has fashioned our psychology of motives ever since. Our map or general theory of the mind may be Freud's, but Freud, like all the rest of us, inherits the representation of mind, at its most subtle and excellent, from Shakespeare. Freud could say that the aim of all life was death, but not that readiness is all, or even that the passing of the Oedipus complex depended upon moving from the image of the dead father to the image of all mortality. When Yorick's skull replaces the helmeted ghost, then the mature Hamlet has replaced the self-chastising revenger and a different sense of death's power over life has been created—and in more than a play or a dramatic poem:

> *Hamlet.*   To what base uses we may return, Horatio! Why may not imagination trace the noble dust of Alexander till 'a find it stopping a bung-hole?
> *Horatio.*   'Twere to consider too curiously to consider so.
> *Hamlet.*   No, faith, not a jot, but to follow him thither with modesty enough, and likelihood to lead it.

Probability leads possibility, likelihood beckons imagination on, and Alexander is essentially a surrogate for the dead father, the Danish Alexander. Passionately reductive, Hamlet would consign his own dust to the same likelihood, but there we part from him, with Horatio as our own surrogate. Hamlet's unique praise of Horatio sets forever the paradigm of the Shakespearean reader or playgoer in relation to the Shakespearean tragic hero:

> Dost thou hear?
> Since my dear soul was mistress of her choice,
> And could of men distinguish her election,
> Sh'ath seal'd thee for herself; for thou hast been
> As one, in suff'ring all, that suffers nothing . . .

Which means not that Horatio and the reader do not suffer with Hamlet, but rather that they truly suffer nothing precisely because they learn from Hamlet the disinterestedness they themselves cannot exemplify, although in possibility somehow share. And they survive, to tell Hamlet's story "of accidental judgments" not so accidental and perhaps not judgments, since disinterestedness does not judge and there are no accidents.

Only Hamlet, at the last, is disinterested, since the hero we see in Act V, despite his protestations, is now beyond love; which is not to say that he never loved Gertrude, or Ophelia, or the dead father, or poor Yorick for that matter. Hamlet is an actor? Yes, earlier, but not in Act V, where he has ceased also to be a play director, and finally even abandons the profession of poet. Language, so dominant as such in the earlier Hamlet, gives almost the illusion of transparency in his last speech, if only because he verges upon saying what cannot be said:

> You that look pale and tremble at this chance,
> That are but mutes or audience to this act,
> Had I but time—as this fell sergeant, Death,

Is strict in his arrest—O, I could tell you—
But let it be.

Evidently he does know something of what he leaves, and
we ache to know what he could tell us, since it is Shakespeare's
power to persuade us that Hamlet has gained a crucial knowledge. One clue is the abiding theatrical trope of "but mutes or
audience," which suggests that the knowledge is itself "of" illusion. But the trope is framed by two announcements to
Horatio and so to us. "I am dead," and no other figure in
Shakespeare seems to stand so authoritatively on the threshold
between the worlds of life and death. When the hero's last
speech moves between "O, I die, Horatio" and "the rest is silence," there is a clear sense again that much more might be
said, concerning our world and not the "undiscovered country" of death. The hint is that Hamlet could tell us something
he has learned about the nature of representation, because he
has learned what it is that he himself represents.

Shakespeare gives Fortinbras the last word on this, but that
word is irony, since Fortinbras exemplifies only the formula of
repetition: like father, like son. "The soldier's music and the
rite of war" speak loudly for the dead father, but not for this
dead son, who had watched the army of Fortinbras march past
to gain its little patch of ground and had mused: "Rightly to be
great / Is not to stir without great argument." The reader's last
word has to be Horatio's, who more truly than Fortinbras has
Hamlet's dying voice: "and from his mouth whose voice will
draw on more," which only in a lesser way means draw more
supporters to the election of Fortinbras. Horatio represents
the audience, while Fortinbras exemplifies all the dead fathers.

We love Hamlet then for whatever reasons Horatio loves
him. Of Horatio we know that what best distinguishes him
from Rosencrantz and Guildenstern, and indeed from Polo-

nius, Ophelia, Laertes—indeed from Gertrude—is that Claudius cannot use him. Critics have remarked upon Horatio's ambiguously shifting status at the court of Denmark, and the late William Empson confessed a certain irritation at Hamlet's discovery of virtues in Horatio that the prince could not find in himself. Yet Shakespeare gives us a Hamlet we must love while knowing our inferiority, since he has the qualities we lack, and so he also gives us Horatio, our representative, who loves so stoically for the rest of us. Horatio is loyal, and limited; skeptical, as befits a fellow student of the profoundly skeptical Hamlet, yet never skeptical about Hamlet. Take Horatio out of the play and you take us out of the play. The plot could be rearranged to spare the wretched Rosencrantz and Guildenstern, even to spare Laertes, let alone Fortinbras; but remove Horatio, and Hamlet becomes so estranged from us that we scarcely can hope to account for that universality of appeal which is his, and the play's, most original characteristic.

Horatio then represents by way of our positive association with him; it is a commonplace, but not less true for that, to say that Hamlet represents by negation. I think this negation is biblical in origin, which is why it seems so Freudian to us, because Freudian negation is biblical and not Hegelian, as it were. Hamlet is biblical rather than Homeric or Sophoclean. Like the Hebrew hero confronting Yahweh, Hamlet needs to be everything in himself yet knows the sense in which he is nothing in himself. What Hamlet takes back from repression is returned only cognitively, never affectively, so that in him thought is liberated from its sexual past, but at the high expense of a continued and augmenting sense of sexual disgust. And what Hamlet at first loves is what biblical and Freudian man loves: the image of authority, the dead father, and the object of the dead father's love, who is also the object of Claudius's love. When Hamlet matures, or returns fully to himself, he transcends the love of authority and ceases to love at all, and perhaps he can be said to be dying throughout all of Act V, and not just in the scene of the duel.

In Freud, we love authority but authority does not love us in return. Nowhere in the play are we told, by Hamlet or by anyone else, of the love of the dead king for his son, but only for Gertrude. That Hamlet hovers always beyond our comprehension must be granted, yet he is not so far beyond as to cause us to see him with the vision of Fortinbras rather than the vision of Horatio. We think of him not necessarily as royal but more as noble, in the archaic sense of "noble," which is to be a seeing soul. It is surely no accident that Horatio is made to emphasize the word "noble" in his elegy for Hamlet, which contrasts angelic song to the "soldier's music" of Fortinbras. As a noble or seeing heart, Hamlet indeed sees feelingly. Short of T. S. Eliot's judgment that the play is an aesthetic failure, the oddest opinion in the *Hamlet* criticism of our time was that of W. H. Auden in his Ibsen essay, "Genius and Apostle," which contrasts Hamlet as a mere actor to Don Quixote as the antithesis of an actor:

> Hamlet lacks faith in God and in himself. Consequently he must define his existence in terms of others, e.g., I am the man whose mother married his uncle who murdered his father. He would like to become what the Greek tragic hero is, a creature of situation. Hence his inability to act, for he can only "act," i.e., play at possibilities.

Harold Goddard, whose *The Meaning of Shakespeare* (1951) seems to me still the most illuminating single book on Shakespeare, remarked that "Hamlet is his own Falstaff." In Goddard's spirit, I might venture the formula: Brutus plus Falstaff equals Hamlet, though "equals" is hardly an accurate word there. A better formula was proposed by A. C. Bradley, when he suggested that Hamlet was the only Shakespearean character who we could think had written Shakespeare's plays. Goddard built on this by saying of Shakespeare: "He is an unfallen Hamlet." From a scholarly or any formalist perspective, Goddard's aphorism is not criticism, but neither historical research nor formalist modes of criticism have helped us much in learning to describe the unassimilated originality that Shakespearean representation still constitutes. Because we are formed by Shakespeare, paradoxically most fully where we cannot assimilate him, we are a little blinded by what might be called the originality of this originality. Only a few critics (A. D. Nuttall among them) have seen that the central element in this originality is its cognitive power. Without Shakespeare we would not know of a literary representation that worked so as to compel reality to reveal aspects of itself that we otherwise could not discern.

Harry Levin, for whom strong misreading is not serendipity but misfortune, advises us that "Hamlet without *Hamlet* has been thought about all too much." One might reply, in all mildness, that little memorable has been written about *Hamlet* that does not fall into the mode of "Hamlet without *Hamlet*." Far more even than *Lear* or *Macbeth,* the play is the figure; the question of *Hamlet* only can be Hamlet. He does not move in a sublime cosmos and truly has no world except himself, which would appear to be what he has learned in the interim between Acts IV and V. Changelings who move from fantasy to fact are possible only in romance, and alas Shakespeare wrote the tragedy of Hamlet and not the romance of Hamlet instead. But the originality of Shakespearean representation in tragedy, and particularly in *Hamlet,* hardly can be overstressed. Shakespeare's version of the family romance always compounds it with two other paradigms for his exuberant originality: with a catastrophe that creates and with a carrying across from earlier ambivalences within the audience to an ambivalence that is a kind of taboo settling in about the tragic hero like an aura. At the close of *Hamlet,* only Horatio and Fortinbras are survivors. Fortinbras presumably will be another warrior-king of Denmark. Horatio does not go home with us, but vanishes into the aura of Hamlet's after-light, perhaps to serve as witness of Hamlet's story over and over again. The hero leaves us with a sense that finally he has fathered himself, that he was beyond our touch though not beyond our affections, and that the catastrophes he helped provoke have brought about not a new creation but a fresh revelation of what was latent in reality yet not evident without his own disaster.

Dr. Samuel Johnson found in the representation of Othello, Iago, and Desdemona "such proofs of Shakespeare's skill in human nature, as, I suppose, it is vain to seek in any modern writer." The high Romantic Victor Hugo gave us the contrary formula: "Next to God, Shakespeare created most," which seems to me not a remystification of Shakespeare's characters but rather a shrewd hint in what might be called the pragmatics of aesthetics. Shakespeare was a mortal god (as Hugo aspired to be) because his art was not a mimesis at all. A mode of representation that is always out ahead of any historically unfolding reality necessarily contains us more than we can contain it. A. D. Nuttall remarks of Iago that he "chooses which emotions he will experience. He is not just motivated, like other people. Instead he *decides* to be motivated." Though Nuttall says that makes of Iago a Camus-like existentialist, I would think Iago is closer to a god, or a devil, and so perhaps resembles his creator, who evidently chose emotions to be experienced, and decided whether or not to be motivated. We do not feel Othello to be a critique of Shakespeare, but in some sense Iago is just that, being a playwright, like Edmund in *King Lear,* like Hamlet, and like William Shakespeare. Hamlet's "the rest is silence" has a curious parallel in Iago's "From this time forth I never will speak word," even though Hamlet dies immediately, and Iago survives to die mutely under torture.

It is not that Iago is in Hamlet's class as an intellectual consciousness. No, Iago is comparable to Edmund, who in *King Lear* out-plots everyone else in the royal world of the play. Othello is a glorious soldier and a sadly simple man, who could be ruined by a villain far less gifted than Iago. A. C. Bradley's charming notion is still true: exchange Othello and Hamlet in one another's plays, and there would be no plays. Othello would chop Claudius down as soon as the ghost had convinced him, and Hamlet would have needed only a few moments to see through Iago, and to begin destroying him by overt parody. But there are no Hamlets, Falstaffs, or inspired clowns in *Othello, the Moor of Venice,* and poor Desdemona is no Portia.

The Moor of Venice is the sometimes neglected part of the tragedy's title. To be the Moor of Venice, its hired general, is an uneasy honor, Venice being then and now the uneasiest of cities. Othello's pigmentation is notoriously essential to the plot. He is hardly a natural man in relation to the subtle Venetians, but the sexual obsessiveness he catches from Iago develops into a dualism that renders him insane. A marvelous monism has yielded to the discontents of Venetian civilization, and we remain haunted by intimations of a different Othello, as though Desdemona, even before Iago's intervention, has been loss as well as gain for the previously integral soldier. Many critics have noted Othello's ruefulness when he speaks in Act I of having exchanged his "unhoused free condition" for his love of "the gentle Desdemona." When we think of him in his glory we remember his ending a street battle with one line of marvelous authority: "Keep up your bright swords, for the dew will rust them." "Sheathe or die" would be the reductive reading, but Othello at his zenith defies reduction, and a fuller interpretation would emphasize the easiness and largeness of this superbly military temperament. How does so spacious and majestic an authority degenerate so rapidly into an equivalent of Spenser's Malbecco? Like Malbecco, Othello forgets he is a man and his name in effect becomes Jealousy. Jealousy in Hawthorne becomes Satan, after having been Chillingworth, while in Proust, first Swann and then Marcel become art historians of jealousy, as it were, obsessive scholars desperately searching for every visual detail of betrayal. Freud's delusional jealousy involves repressed homosexuality and seems inapplicable to Othello, though not wholly so to Iago. Jealousy in Shakespeare—parent to its presence in Hawthorne, Proust, and Freud—is a mask for the fear of death, since what the jealous lover fears is that there will not be time or space enough for himself. It is one of the peculiar splendors of *Othello* that we cannot understand Othello's belated jealousy without first understanding Iago's primal envy of Othello, which is at the hidden center of the drama.

Frank Kermode curiously says that "Iago's naturalist ethic . . . is a wicked man's version of Montaigne," a judgment that Ben Jonson might have welcomed, but that I find alien to Shakespeare. Iago is not a naturalist but the fiercest version in all literature of an ideologue of the reductive fallacy, which can be defined as the belief that what is most real about any one of us is the worst thing that possibly could be true of us. "Tell me what she or he is *really* like," the reductionist keeps saying, and means: "Tell me the worst thing you can." Presumably the reductionist cannot bear to be deceived, and so becomes a professional at deception.

Iago is Othello's standard-bearer, a senior officer skilled and courageous in the field, as we have every reason to believe. "I am not what I am" is his chilling motto, endless to meditation, which only superficially echoes Saint Paul's "I am what I am." "I am that I am" is God's name in answer to the query of

Moses, and reverberates darkly and antithetically in "I am not what I am." God will be where and when He will be, present or absent as is His choice. Iago is the spirit that will not be, the spirit of absence, a pure negativity. We know therefore from the start why Iago hates Othello, who is the largest presence, the fullest being in Iago's world, particularly in battle. The hatred pretends to be empirical, but is ontological, and consequently unquenchable. If Platonic eros is the desire for what one hasn't got, then Iago's hatred is the drive to destroy what one hasn't got. We shudder when the maddened Othello vows death to Desdemona as a "fair devil" and promotes Iago to be his lieutenant, for Iago superbly responds "I am your own for ever," and means the reverse: "You too are now an absence."

Step by step, Iago falls into his own gap of being, changing as he hears himself plot, improvising a drama that must destroy the dramatist as well as his protagonists:

> And what's he then that says I play the villain,
> When this advice is free I give, and honest,
> Probal to thinking, and indeed the course
> To win the Moor again? For 'tis most easy
> Th' inclining Desdemona to subdue
> In any honest suit; she's fram'd as fruitful
> As the free elements. And then for her
> To win the Moor, were't to renounce his baptism,
> All seals and symbols of redeemed sin,
> His soul is so enfetter'd to her love,
> That she may make, unmake, do what she list,
> Even as her appetite shall play the god
> With his weak function. How am I then a villain,
> To counsel Cassio to this parallel course,
> Directly to his good? Divinity of hell!
> When devils will the blackest sins put on,
> They do suggest at first with heavenly shows,
> As I do now; for whiles this honest fool
> Plies Desdemona to repair his fortune,

And she for him pleads strongly to the Moor,
I'll pour this pestilence into his ear—
That she repeals him for her body's lust,
And by how much she strives to do him good,
She shall undo her credit with the Moor.
So will I turn her virtue into pitch,
And out of her own goodness make the net
That shall enmesh them all.

Harold C. Goddard called Iago a "moral pyromaniac," and
we can hear Iago setting fire to himself throughout the play,
but particularly in this speech. I think that Goddard, a profoundly imaginative critic, trapped the essence of Iago when
he saw that Iago was always at war, making every encounter,
every moment, into an act of destruction. War is the ultimate
reductive fallacy, since to kill your enemy you must believe the
worst that can be believed about him. What changes in Iago as
he listens to himself is that he loses perspective, because his
rhetoric isolates by burning away context. Isolation, Freud
tells us, is the compulsive's guarantee that the coherence of his
thinking will not be interrupted. Iago interposes intervals of
monologue so as to defend himself against his own awareness
of change in himself, and thus ironically intensifies his own
change into the totally diabolic. Like the monologues of Shakespeare's Richard III, Iago's monologues are swerves away from
the divine "I am that I am," past "I am not what I am," on to "I
am not," negation mounting to an apotheosis.

The collapse of Othello is augmented in dignity and poignance when we gain our full awareness of Iago's achieved
negativity, war everlasting. No critic need judge Othello to be
stupid, for Othello does not incarnate war, being as he is a
sane and honorable warrior. He is peculiarly vulnerable to
Iago precisely because Iago is his standard-bearer, the protec-
tor of his colors and reputation in battle, pledged to die rather

than allow the colors to be taken. His equivalent to Iago's monologues is a stirring elegy for the self, a farewell to war as a valid because confined occupation:

I had been happy, if the general camp,
Pioners and all, had tasted her sweet body,
So I had nothing known. O now, for ever
Farewell the tranquil mind! farewell content!
Farewell the plumed troops and the big wars
That makes ambition virtue! O, farewell!
Farewell the neighing steed and the shrill trump,
The spirit-stirring drum, th' ear-piercing fife,
The royal banner, and all quality,
Pride, pomp, and circumstance of glorious war!
And O you mortal engines, whose rude throats
Th' immortal Jove's dread clamors counterfeit,
Farewell! Othello's occupation's gone.

"Pride, pomp, and circumstance of glorious war" has yielded to Iago's incessant war against being. Othello, within his occupation's limits, has the greatness of the tragic hero. Iago breaks down those limits from within, from war's own camp, and so Othello has no chance. Had the attack come from the world outside war's dominion, Othello could have maintained some coherence, and gone down in the name of the purity of arms. Shakespeare, courting a poetics of pain, could not allow his hero that consolation. Othello, unlike Iago, has no biblical context to give him coherence, however negative. Shakespeare shrewdly went on to give Lear that context, by subtly invoking the Book of Job.

❧

A comparison between the disasters of Job and of Lear is likely to lead to some startling conclusions about the preternatural persuasiveness of Shakespearean representation, an art whose limits we have yet to discover. This art convinces us that Lear exposed to the storm, out on the heath, is a designedly Jobean figure. To fall from king of Britain to a fugitive in the open, pelted by merciless weather and betrayed by ungrateful daughters, is indeed an unpleasant fate, but is it truly Jobean? Job, after all, experiences an even more dreadful sublimity; his sons, daughters, servants, sheep, camels, and houses are all destroyed by satanic fires, and his direct physical torment far transcends Lear's—not to mention that he still suffers his wife, while we never do hear anything about Lear's queen, who amazingly brought forth monsters of the deep, in Goneril and Regan, but also Cordelia, a soul in bliss. What would Lear's wife have said, had she accompanied her royal husband onto the heath? Not, in any case, what Job's wife utters, in the Geneva Bible: "Doest thou continue yet in thine uprightnes? Blaspheme God, and dye."

That Shakespeare intended his audience to see Job as the model for Lear's situation (though hardly for Lear himself) seems likely, on the basis of a pattern of allusions in the drama. Imagery that associates humans with worms, and with dust, is strikingly present in both works. Lear himself presumably thinks of Job when he desperately asserts: "I will be the pattern of all patience," a dreadful irony considering the king's ferociously impatient nature. Job is the righteous man handed over to the Accuser, but Lear is a blind king who knows neither himself nor his daughters. Though Lear suffers the storm's fury, he is not Job-like either in his earlier sufferings (which he greatly magnifies), or in his relationship to the divine. It is another indication of Shakespeare's strong originality that he persuades us of the Jobean dignity and grandeur of Lear's first sufferings, even though to a considerable degree they are brought about by Lear himself, in sharp contrast to Job's absolute blamelessness. When Lear says that he is a man more sinned against than sinning, we tend to believe him, but is this really true at that point?

It is true only proleptically, in prophecy—but again this is Shakespeare's astonishing originality, founded upon the representation of impending change, a change to be worked within Lear by his own listening to, and reflecting upon, what he himself speaks aloud in his increasing fury. He goes into the storm scene on the heath still screaming in anger, goes mad with that anger, and comes out of the storm with crucial change deeply in process within him, full of paternal love for the fool and concern for the supposed madman, Edgar impersonating Poor Tom. Lear's constant changes from then until the terrible end remain the most remarkable representation of a human transformation anywhere in imaginative literature.

But why did Shakespeare risk the paradigm of Job, since Lear, early and late, is so unlike Job, and since the play is anything but a theodicy? Milton remarked that the Book of Job was the rightful model for a "brief epic," such as his *Paradise Regained,* but in what sense can it be an appropriate model for a tragedy? Shakespeare may have been pondering his setting of *King Lear* in a Britain seven centuries before the time of Christ, a placement historically earlier than he attempted anywhere else, except for the Trojan War of *Troilus and Cressida. Lear* presumably is not a Christian play, though Cordelia is an eminently Christian personage who says that she is about her father's business, in an overt allusion to the Gospels. But the Christian God and Jesus Christ are not relevant to the cosmos of *King Lear.* So appalling is the tragedy of this tragedy that Shakespeare shrewdly sets it before the Christian dispensation, in what he may have intuited was the time of Job. If *Macbeth* is Shakespeare's one full-scale venture into a Gnostic cosmos (and I think it was), then *King Lear* risks a more complete and catastrophic tragedy than anything in the genre before or since.

Job, rather oddly, ultimately receives the reward of his virtue, but Lear, purified and elevated, suffers instead the horror of Cordelia's murder by the underlings of Edmund. I think, then, that Shakespeare invoked the Book of Job in order to emphasize the absolute negativity of Lear's tragedy. Had Lear's wife been alive, she would have done well to emulate Job's wife and advise her husband to blaspheme God and die. Pragmatically, it would have been a better fate than the one Lear finally suffers in the play.

The Gloucester subplot may be said to work deliberately against Lear's Jobean sense of his own uniqueness as a sufferer; his tragedy will not be the one he desires, for it is a tragedy not so much of filial ingratitude as of a kind of apocalyptic nihilism, universal in its implications. We do not sympathize with Lear's immense curses, though they are increasingly related to his rising fear of madness, which is also his fear of a womanly nature rising up within him. Finally Lear's madness, like his curses, proceeds from his biblical sense of himself; desiring to be everything in himself, he fears greatly that he is nothing. His obsession with his own blindness seems related to an aging vitalist's fear of impotence, and so of mortality. Yet Lear is not just any old hero, nor even just a great king falling away into madness and death. Shakespeare allows him a diction more preternaturally eloquent than is spoken by anyone else in this or any other drama, and that evidently never will be matched again. Lear matters because his language is uniquely strong, and because we are persuaded that this splendor is wholly appropriate to him.

Nature, in the drama, is both origin and end, mother and catastrophe, and it ought to be Lear's function to hold and safeguard the middle ground between the daemonic world and the realm of the gods. He fails, massively, and the ensuing tragedy engulfs an entire world, with a poignance unmatched in literature.

Enter LEAR [*mad, crowned with weeds and flowers*].

[*Edgar.*] But who comes here?
The safer sense will ne'er accommodate
His master thus.

Lear. No, they cannot touch me for coining, I am the King himself.

Edgar. O thou side-piercing sight!

Lear. Nature's above art in that respect. There's your press-money. That fellow handles his bow like a crow-keeper; draw me a clothier's yard. Look, look, a mouse! Peace, peace, this piece of toasted cheese will do't. There's my gauntlet, I'll prove it on a giant. Bring up the brown bills. O, well flown, bird! i' th' clout, i' th' clout—hewgh! Give the word.

Edgar. Sweet marjorum.

Lear. Pass.

Gloucester. I know that voice.

Lear. Ha! Goneril with a white beard? They flatter'd me like a dog, and told me I had the white hairs in my beard ere the black ones were there. To say "ay" and "no" to every thing that I said! "Ay," and "no" too, was no good divinity. When the rain came to wet me once, and the wind to make me chatter, when the thunder would not peace at my bidding, there I found 'em, there I smelt 'em out. Go to, they are not men o' their words: they told me I was every thing. 'Tis a lie, I am not ague-proof.

Gloucester. The trick of that voice I do well remember; Is't not the King?

Lear. Ay, every inch a king!
When I do stare, see how the subject quakes.
I pardon that man's life. What was thy cause?
Adultery?
Thou shalt not die. Die for adultery? No,
The wren goes to't, and the small gilded fly
Does lecher in my sight.
Let copulation thrive; for Gloucester's bastard son
Was kinder to his father than my daughters
Got 'tween the lawful sheets.
To't, luxury, pell-mell, for I lack soldiers.

Behold yond simp'ring dame,
Whose face between her forks presages snow;
That minces virtue, and does shake the head
To hear of pleasure's name—
The fitchew nor the soiled horse goes to't
With a more riotous appetite.
Down from the waist they are Centaurs,
Though women all above;
But to the girdle do the gods inherit,
Beneath is all the fiends': there's hell, there's darkness,
There is the sulphurous pit, burning, scalding,
Stench, consumption. Fie, fie, fie! pah, pah!
Give me an ounce of civet; good apothecary,
Sweeten my imagination. There's money for thee.

    Gloucester.   O, let me kiss that hand!

    Lear.   Let me wipe it first, it smells of mortality.

    Gloucester.   O ruin'd piece of nature! This great world
Shall so wear out to nought. Dost thou know me?

    Lear.   I remember thine eyes well enough. Dost thou
squiny at me? No, do thy worst, blind Cupid, I'll not love. Read
thou this challenge; mark but the penning of it.

    Gloucester.   Were all thy letters suns, I could not see.

    Edgar.   [*Aside.*] I would not take this from report; it is,
And my heart breaks at it.

    Lear.   Read.

    Gloucester.   What, with the case of eyes?

    Lear.   O ho, are you there with me? No eyes in your head,
nor no money in your purse? Your eyes are in a heavy case, your
purse in a light, yet you see how this world goes.

    Gloucester.   I see it feelingly.

    Lear.   What, art mad? A man may see how this world goes
with no eyes. Look with thine ears; see how yond justice rails
upon yond simple thief. Hark in thine ear: change places, and
handy-dandy, which is the justice, which is the thief? Thou hast
seen a farmer's dog bark at a beggar?

    Gloucester.   Ay, sir.

    Lear.   And the creature run from the cur? There thou

mightst behold the great image of authority: a dog's obey'd in
office.
Thou rascal beadle, hold thy bloody hand!
Why dost thou lash that whore? Strip thy own back,
Thou hotly lusts to use her in that kind
For which thou whip'st her. The usurer hangs the cozener.
Thorough tatter'd clothes small vices do appear;
Robes and furr'd gowns hide all. Plate sin with gold,
And the strong lance of justice hurtless breaks;
Arm it in rags, a pigmy's straw does pierce it.
None does offend, none, I say none, I'll able 'em.
Take that of me, my friend, who have the power
To seal th' accuser's lips. Get thee glass eyes,
And like a scurvy politician, seem
To see the things thou dost not. Now, now, now, now.
Pull off my boots; harder, harder—so.
    Edgar.   [*Aside.*] O, matter and impertinency mix'd,
Reason in madness!
    Lear.   If thou wilt weep my fortunes, take my eyes.
I know thee well enough, thy name is Gloucester.
Thou must be patient; we came crying hither.
Thou know'st, the first time that we smell the air
We wawl and cry. I will preach to thee. Mark.
    [*Lear takes off his crown of weeds and flowers.*]
    Gloucester.   Alack, alack the day!
    Lear.   When we are born, we cry that we are come
To this great stage of fools.—This' a good block.
It were a delicate stratagem, to shoe
A troop of horse with felt. I'll put't in proof,
And when I have stol'n upon these son-in-laws,
Then kill, kill, kill, kill, kill, kill!

Kermode justly remarks of this scene that it is at once Shakespeare's boldest effort of imagination and utterly lacking in
narrative function. Indeed, it strictly lacks all function, and the
tragedy does not need it. We do not reason the need: poetic

language never has gone further. Edgar, who once pretended madness, begins by observing that "the safer sense" or sane mind cannot accommodate itself to the vision of the ultimate paternal authority having gone mad. But "safer sense" here also refers to seeing, and the entire scene is a vastation organized about the dual images of eyesight and of fatherhood, images linked yet also severed throughout the play. The sight that pierces Edgar's side is intolerable to a quiet hero whose only quest has been to preserve the image of his father's authority. His father, blinded Gloucester, recognizing authority by its voice, laments the mad king as nature's ruined masterpiece, and prophesies that a similar madness will wear away the entire world into nothingness. The prophecy will be fulfilled in the drama's closing scene, but is deferred so that the reign of "reason in Madness" or sight in blindness can be continued. Pathos transcends all limits in Lear's great and momentary breakthrough to sanity, as he cries out to Gloucester, and to all of us: "If thou wilt weep my fortune, take my eyes."

Hardly the pattern of all patience, Lear nevertheless has earned the convincing intensity of telling Gloucester "Thou must be patient." What follows however is not Jobean but a Shakespearean version of the Wisdom of Solomon 7:3 and 6 ("When I was born, I breathed the common air and was laid on the earth that all men tread; and the first sound I uttered, as all do, was a cry . . . for all come into life by a single path, and by a single path go out again"). It holds the essence of the drama's prophecy: "we came crying hither" and "When we are born, we cry that we are come / To this great stage of fools." That great theatrical trope encompasses every meaning the play crams into the word "fool": actor, moral being, idealist, child, dear one, madman, victim, truth-teller. As Northrop Frye observes, the only characters in *King Lear* who are not fools are Edmund, Goneril, Regan, Cornwall and their followers.

Lear's own Fool undergoes a subtle transformation as the

drama burns on, from an oracle of forbidden wisdom to a frightened child, until at last he simply disappears, as though he blent into the identity of the dead Cordelia when the broken Lear cries out: "And my poor fool is hang'd!" Subtler still is the astonishing transformation of the most interesting consciousness in the play, the bastard Edmund, Shakespeare's most intensely theatrical villain, surpassing even Richard III and Iago. Edmund, as theatrical as Barabas, Marlowe's Jew of Malta, might almost be a sly portrait of Christopher Marlowe himself. As the purest and coolest Machiavel in stage history, at least until he knows he has received his death wound, Edmund is both a remarkably antic and charming Satan and a being with real self-knowledge, which makes him particularly dangerous in a world presided over by Lear, "who hath ever but slenderly known himself," as Regan remarks.

Edmund's mysterious and belated metamorphosis as the play nears its end, a movement from playing oneself to being oneself, turns upon his complex reactions to his own deathly musing, "Yet Edmund was beloved." It is peculiarly shocking and pathetic that his lovers were Goneril and Regan, monsters who proved their love by suicide and murder, but Shakespeare seems to have wished to give us a virtuoso display of his original art in changing character through the representation of a growing inwardness. Outrageously refreshing at his most evil (Edgar is a virtuous bore in contrast to him), Edmund is the most attractive of Jacobean hero-villains, and inevitably captures both Goneril and Regan, evidently with singularly little effort. His dangerous attractiveness is one of the principal unexplored clues to the enigmas of Shakespeare's most sublime achievement. That Edmund has gusto, an exuberance befitting his role as natural son, is merely part of the given. His intelligence and will are more central to him, and darken the meanings of *King Lear*.

Wounded to death by Edgar, his brother, Edmund yields to

fortune: "The wheel is come full circle, I am here." Where he is not is upon Lear's "wheel of fire," in a place of saving madness. Not only do Edmund and Lear exchange not a single word in the course of this vast drama, but it defies imagination to conceive of what they could say to one another. It is not only the intricacies of the double plot that keep Edmund and Lear apart; they have no language in common. Frye points out that "nature" takes on antithetical meanings in Lear and Edmund, in regard to the other, and this can be expanded to the realization that Lear, despite all his faults, is incapable of guile, but Edmund is incapable of an honest passion of any kind. The lover of both Goneril and Regan, he is passive toward both, and is moved by their deaths only to reflect upon what is for him the extraordinary reality that anyone, however monstrous, ever should have loved him at all.

Why does he reform, however belatedly, and ineffectually, since Cordelia is murdered anyway; what are we to make of his final turn toward the light? Edmund's first reaction to the news of the deaths of Goneril and Regan is the grimly dispassionate "I was contracted to them both; all three / Now marry in an instant," which identifies dying and marrying as a single act. In the actual moment of repentance, Edmund desperately says: "I pant for life. Some good I mean to do, / Despite of my own nature." This is not to say that nature no longer is his goddess, but rather that he is finally touched by images of connection or concern, be they as far apart as Edgar's care for Gloucester, or Goneril's and Regan's fiercely competitive lust for his own person.

I conclude by returning to my fanciful speculation that the Faustian Edmund is not only overtly Marlovian, but indeed may be Shakespeare's charmed but wary portrait of elements in Christopher Marlowe himself. Edmund represents the way not to go, and yet is the only figure in *King Lear* who is truly at home in its apocalyptic cosmos. The wheel comes full circle for him, but he has limned his night-piece, and it was his best.

Falstaff is to the world of the histories what Hamlet is to the tragedies, *the* problematical representation. Falstaff and Hamlet put to us the question: precisely how does Shakespearean representation differ from anything before it, and how has it overdetermined our expectations of representation ever since? The fortunes of Falstaff in scholarship and criticism have been almost endlessly dismal, and I will not resume them here. I prefer Harold Goddard on Falstaff to any other commentator, and yet I am aware that Goddard appears to have sentimentalized and even idealized Falstaff. Better that than the endless litany absurdly patronizing Falstaff as Vice, Parasite, Fool, Braggart Soldier, Corrupt Glutton, Seducer of Youth, Cowardly Liar, and everything else that would not earn the greatest wit in all literature an honorary degree at Yale or a place on the board of the Ford Foundation.

Falstaff, in Shakespeare rather than in Verdi, is precisely what Nietzsche tragically attempted yet failed to represent in his Zarathustra: a person without a superego, or, should I say, Socrates without the *daimon*. Perhaps even better, Falstaff is not the Sancho Panza of Cervantes but the exemplary figure of Kafka's parable "The Truth about Sancho Panza." Kafka's Sancho Panza, a free man, has diverted his *daimon* from him by many nightly feedings of chivalric romances (it would be science fiction nowadays). Diverted from Sancho, his true object, the *daimon* becomes the harmless Don Quixote, whose mishaps prove edifying entertainment for the "philosophic" Sancho, who proceeds to follow his errant *daimon* out of a sense of responsibility. Falstaff's "failure," if it can be termed that, is that he fell in love not with his own *daimon* but with

his bad son, Hal, who all too truly turned out to be Boling-
broke's son. The witty knight should have diverted his own
daimon with Shakespearean comedies, and philosophically
have followed the *daimon* off to the forest of Arden.

Falstaff is neither good enough nor bad enough to flourish
in the world of the histories. But then he is necessarily beyond
not only good and evil but cause and effect as well. A greater
monist than the young Milton, Falstaff plays at dualism partly
in order to mock all dualisms, whether Christian, Platonic or
even the Freudian dualism that he both anticipates and in
some sense refutes.

Falstaff provoked the best of all critics, Dr. Johnson, into the
judgment that "he has nothing in him that can be esteemed."
George Bernard Shaw, perhaps out of envy, called Falstaff "a
besotted and disgusting old wretch." Yet Falstaff's sole rival
in Shakespeare is Hamlet; no one else, as Oscar Wilde noted,
has so comprehensive a consciousness. Representation itself
changed permanently because of Hamlet and Falstaff. I begin
with my personal favorite among all of Falstaff's remarks, if
only because I plagiarize it daily: "O, thou hast damnable
iteration, and art indeed able to corrupt a saint: thou hast
done much harm upon me, Hal, God forgive thee for it: before I knew thee, Hal, I knew nothing, and now am I, if a man
should speak truly, little better than one of the wicked."

W. H. Auden, whose Falstaff essentially was Verdi's, believed the knight to be "a comic symbol for the supernatural
order of charity," and thus a displacement of Christ into the
world of wit. The charm of this reading, though considerable,
neglects Falstaff's grandest quality, his immanence. He is as
immanent a representation as Hamlet is transcendent. Better
than any formulation of Freud's, Falstaff perpetually shows us
that the ego indeed is always a bodily ego. And the bodily ego
is always vulnerable, and Hal indeed has done much harm
upon it, and will do far worse, and will need forgiveness,

though no sensitive audience ever will forgive him. Falstaff, like Hamlet, and like Lear's Fool, does speak truly, and Falstaff remains, despite Hal, rather better than one of the wicked, or the good.

For what is supreme immanence in what might be called the order of representation? This is another way of again asking: is not Falstaff, like Hamlet, so original a representation that he originates much of what we know or expect about representation? We cannot see how original Falstaff is, because Falstaff contains us; we do not contain him. And though we love Falstaff, he does not need our love, any more than Hamlet does. His sorrow is that he loves Hal rather more than Hamlet loves Ophelia, or even Gertrude. The Hamlet of Act V is past loving anyone, but that is a gift (if it is a gift) resulting from transcendence. If you dwell wholly in this world, and if you are, as Falstaff is, a pervasive entity, or, as Freud would say, "a strong egoism," then you must begin to love, as Freud also says, in order that you may not fall ill. But what if your strong egoism is not afflicted by any ego-ideal, what if you are never watched, or watched over, by what is above the ego? Falstaff is *not* subject to a power that watches, discovers and criticizes all his intentions. Falstaff, except for his single and misplaced love, is free, is freedom itself, because he seems free of the superego.

Why does Falstaff (and not his parody in *The Merry Wives of Windsor*) pervade histories rather than comedies? To begin is to be free, and you cannot begin freshly in comedy, any more than you can in tragedy. Both genres are family romances, at least in Shakespeare. History, in Shakespeare, is hardly the genre of freedom for kings and nobles, but it is for Falstaff. How and why? Falstaff is of course his own mother and his own father, begotten out of wit by caprice. Ideally he wants nothing except the audience, which he always has; who could watch anyone else on stage when Ralph Richardson was playing Falstaff? Not so ideally, he evidently wants the love of a son, and invests in Hal, the impossible object. But primarily he has what he must have, the audience's fascination with the ultimate image of freedom. His precursor in Shakespeare is not Puck or Bottom, but Faulconbridge the Bastard in *The Life and Death of King John*. Each has a way of providing a daemonic chorus that renders silly all royal and noble squabbles and intrigues. The Bastard in *King John,* forthright like his father Richard the Lion Heart, is not a wicked wit, but his truth-telling brutally prophesies Falstaff's function.

There are very nearly as many Falstaffs as there are critics, which probably is as it should be. These proliferating Falstaffs tend to be either degraded or idealized, again perhaps inevitably. One of the most ambiguous Falstaffs was created by the late William Empson: "he is the scandalous upper-class man whose behavior embarrasses his class and thereby pleases the lower class in the audience, as an 'exposure.'" To Empson, Falstaff also was both nationalist and Machiavel, "and he had a dangerous amount of power." Empson shared the hint of Wyndham Lewis that Falstaff was homosexual and so presumably lusted (doubtless in vain) after Hal. To complete this portrait, Empson added that Falstaff, being both an aristocrat and a mob leader, was "a familiar dangerous type," a sort of Alcibiades, one presumes.

Confronted by so ambiguous a Falstaff, I return to the sublime knight's rhetoric, which I read very differently, since Falstaff's power seems to me not at all a matter of class, sexuality, politics, nationalism. Power it is: sublime pathos, *potentia,* the drive for life, more life, at any and every cost. I will propose that Falstaff is neither a noble synecdoche nor a grand hyperbole, but rather a metalepsis or farfetcher, to use Puttenham's term. To exist without a superego is to be a solar trajectory, an ever-early brightness, which Nietzsche's Zarathustra, in his bathos, failed to be. "Try to live as though it were morning," Nietzsche advises. Falstaff does not need the advice, as we discover when we first encounter him:

> *Falstaff.* Now, Hal, what time of day is it, lad?
> *Prince.* Thou art so fat-witted with drinking of old sack, and unbuttoning thee after supper, and sleeping upon benches after noon, that thou hast forgotten to demand that truly which thou wouldst truly know. What a devil hast thou to do with the time of day? Unless hours were cups of sack, and minutes capons, and clocks the tongues of bawds, and dials the signs of leaping-houses, and the blessed sun himself a fair hot wench in flame-coloured taffeta, I see no reason why thou shouldst be so superfluous to demand the time of day.

I take it that wit here remains with Falstaff, who is not only witty in himself but the cause of wit in his ephebe, Prince Hal, who mocks his teacher, but in the teacher's own exuberant manner and mode. Perhaps there is a double meaning when Falstaff opens his reply with "Indeed, you come near me now, Hal," since near is as close as the Prince can come when he imitates the master. Master of what is the crucial question, generally answered so badly. To take up the stance of most Shakespeare scholars is to associate Falstaff with: "such inordinate and low desires, / Such poore, such bare, such lewd, such mean attempts, / Such barren pleasures, rude society." I quote King Henry the Fourth, aggrieved usurper, whose description of Falstaff's aura is hardly recognizable to the audience. We recognize rather: "Counterfeit? I lie, I am no counterfeit; to die is to be a counterfeit, for he is but the counterfeit of a man, who hath not the life of a man: but to counterfeit dying, when a man thereby liveth, is to be no counterfeit, but the true and perfect image of life himself." As Falstaff rightly says, he has saved his life by counterfeiting death, and presumably the moralizing critics would be delighted had the unrespectable knight been butchered by Douglas, "that hot termagant Scot."

The true and perfect image of life, Falstaff, confirms his truth and perfection by counterfeiting dying and so evading death. Though he is given to parodying Puritan preachers, Falstaff has an authentic obsession with the dreadful parable of the rich man and Lazarus in Luke 16. A certain rich man, a purple-clad glutton, is contrasted to the beggar Lazarus, who desired "to be fed with the crumbs which fell from the rich man's table: moreover the dogs came and licked his sores." Both glutton and beggar die, but Lazarus is carried into Abraham's bosom and the purple glutton into hell, from which he cries vainly for Lazarus to come and cool his tongue. Falstaff stares at Bardolph, his Knight of the Burning Lamp, and affirms: "I never see thy face but I think upon hell-fire, and Dives that lived in purple: for there he is in his robes, burning, burning." Confronting his hundred-and-fifty tattered prodigals as he marches them off to be food for powder, Falstaff calls them "slaves as ragged as Lazarus in the painted cloth, where the glutton's dogs licked his sores." In *Henry the Fourth*, Part II, Falstaff's first speech again returns to this fearful text, as he cries out against one who denies him credit: "Let him be damn'd like the glutton! Pray God his tongue be hotter!" Despite the ironies abounding in the invoking of Dives by Falstaff the glutton, Shakespeare reverses the New Testament, and Falstaff ends, like Lazarus—and perhaps like Hamlet—in Abraham's bosom, according to the convincing testimony of Mistress Quickly in *Henry the Fifth*, where Arthur Britishly replaces Abraham: "Nay sure, he's not in hell; he's in Arthur's bosom, if ever man went to Arthur's bosom. 'A made a finer end, and went away and it had been any christom child."

In dying, Falstaff is a newly baptized child, innocent of all stain. The pattern of allusions to Luke suggests a crossing over, with the rejected Falstaff a poor Lazarus upon his knees in front of Dives wearing the royal purple of Henry V. To a moralizing critic, this is outrageous, but Shakespeare does stranger tricks with Biblical texts. Juxtapose the two moments:

Falstaff. My King, My Jove! I speak to thee, my heart!
King. I know thee not, old man, fall to thy prayers.
How ill white hairs becomes a fool and jester!
I have long dreamt of such a kind of man,
So surfeit-swell'd, so old, and so profane;
But being awak'd, I do despise my dream.

And here is Abraham refusing to let Lazarus come to comfort the "clothed in purple" Dives: "And beside all this, between us and you there is a great gulf fixed: so that they which would pass from hence to you cannot: neither can they pass to us, that would come from thence." Wherever Henry V is, he is not in Arthur's bosom with the rejected Falstaff.

I suggest that Shakespearean representation in the histories indeed demands our understanding of what Shakespeare did to history, in contrast to what his contemporaries did. Standard scholarly views of literary history, and all Marxist reductions of literature and history alike, have the curiously allied trait of working very well for, say, Thomas Dekker, but being absurdly irrelevant for Shakespeare. Falstaff and the Tudor theory of kingship? Falstaff and surplus value? I would prefer Falstaff and Nietzsche's vision of the use and abuse of history for life, if it were not that Falstaff triumphs precisely where the Overman fails. One can read Freud on our discomfort in culture backward, and get somewhere close to Falstaff, but the problem again is that Falstaff triumphs precisely where Freud denies that triumph is possible. With Falstaff as with Hamlet (and perhaps with Cleopatra) Shakespearean representation is so self-begotten and so influential that we can apprehend it only by seeing that it originates us. We cannot judge a mode of representation that has overdetermined our ideas of representation. Like only a few other authors—the Yahwist, Chaucer, Cervantes, Tolstoy—Shakespeare calls all recent critiques of literary representation severely into doubt. Jacob, the Pardoner, Sancho Panza, Hadji Murad: it seems absurd to call them figures of rhetoric, let alone to see Falstaff, Hamlet, Shylock, Cleopatra as tropes of ethos or of pathos. Falstaff is not language but diction, the product of Shakespeare's will over language, a will that changes characters through and by what they say. Most simply, again, Falstaff is not how meaning is renewed, but rather how meaning gets started.

Falstaff is so profoundly original a representation because most truly he represents the essence of invention, which is the essence of poetry. He is a perpetual catastrophe, a continuous transference, a universal family romance. If Hamlet is beyond us and beyond our need of him, so that we require our intro-jection of Horatio in order to identify ourselves with Horatio's love for Hamlet, then Falstaff too is beyond us. But in the Falstaffian beyonding, as it were, in what I think we must call the Falstaffian sublimity, we are never permitted by Shake-speare to identify ourselves with the Prince's ambivalent af-fection for Falstaff. Future monarchs have no friends, only followers, and Falstaff, the man without a superego, is no one's follower. Freud never speculated what a person without a superego would be like, perhaps because that had been the dangerous prophecy of Nietzsche's Zarathustra. Is there not some sense in which Falstaff's whole being implicitly says to us: "The wisest among you is also merely a conflict and a hybrid between plant and phantom. But do I bid you become phan-toms or plants?" Historical critics who call Falstaff a phantom, and moral critics who judge Falstaff to be a plant, can be left to be answered by Sir John himself. Even in his debased form in *The Merry Wives of Windsor* he crushes them thus: "Have I liv'd to stand at the taunt of one that makes fritters of English? This is enough to be the decay of lust and late-walking through the realm."

But most of all Falstaff is a reproach to all critics who seek to demystify mimesis, whether by Marxist or deconstructionist dialectics. Like Hamlet, Falstaff is a super-mimesis, and so he too compels us to see aspects of reality we otherwise could never apprehend. Marx would teach us what he calls "the appropriation of human reality" and so the appropriation also of human suffering. Nietzsche and his deconstructionist descendants would teach us the necessary irony of failure in every attempt to represent human reality. Falstaff, being more of an original, teaches us himself: "No, that's certain, I am not a double man; but if I be not Jack Falstaff, then am I a Jack." A double man is either a phantom or two men, and a man who is two men might as well be a plant. Sir John is Jack Falstaff; it is the Prince who is a Jack or rascal, and so are Falstaff's moralizing critics. We are in no position then to judge Falstaff or to assess him as a representation of reality. Hamlet is too dispassionate even to *want* to contain us. Falstaff is passionate, and challenges us not to bore him, if he is to deign to represent us.

IV

MILTON

J OHN MILTON never stumbled about in a cosmological emptiness stretching between truth and meaning. He enjoyed the possession of a rocklike ego, and was persuaded that he incarnated truth, so that his life was rammed with meaning. Belief, for Milton, was the liberty exercised by his own pure and upright heart, while poetry was what he sublimely wrote, in loving but fierce competition with the Bible and Homer, Virgil and Dante, Spenser and Shakespeare. No Western poet, or writer of any kind, is as valuable to us as is Milton at this bad moment, when there is a flight away from poetry in our literary academies, now being converted into temples of societal resentment. Milton's power is not what our current School of Resentment loathes yet purports to study; not social, political, economic power, but rhetorical or psychic strength, poetic power proper. Miltonic power is *potentia*, pathos as the capacity for more life. Blake, Whitman, D. H. Lawrence were heroic vitalists, but compared to Milton they can seem involuntary parodists of his effortless and more sublime vitalism. They were compelled to be programmatic, while mere being provided him with heroic argument.

My overt subject here is Milton's marvelous monism, his refusal of every dualism, whether Platonic, Pauline, or Cartesian. But to speak of monism in Milton is a poor way of speaking, akin to speaking of his heresies, or of his beliefs. The greatest poverty, according to Wallace Stevens, is not to live in a physical world, to feel that one's desire is too difficult to distinguish from despair. Milton's own desire was never to be different, never to be elsewhere; in that Nietzschean sense, Milton had no motive for metaphor. That may be why Milton's actual God is not the figure or representation of God which is *Paradise Lost*'s major blemish, any more than the Yahwist's Yahweh is the God of normative Judaism, or of any branch of Christianity, or of Islam. Let us conceive of John Milton as theomorphic, a kind of mortal god, which is how our high Romantic precursors conceived him. The true God of *Paradise Lost* is the narrator, rather than the Urizenic schoolmaster of souls scolding away on his throne or the Holy Spirit invoked by the Arian Milton, not as part of a Trinity, and not as Milton's muse either, since the muse for Milton is simply his own indwelling power, his interior paramour. Spirit and power are one concept in Milton; they unite in the trope of Messiah, and they come close to uniting dangerously in the figure of Milton himself, not just as the voice speaking the poem, but as the maker of both an older and a newer testament than the testaments already available to him. Dante, like Joachim of Flora, spoke his word as a third revelation. Milton, more outrageously ambitious, spoke his word as a revelation prior even to that of Moses, and necessarily more contemporary than that of every rival whosoever.

Our weak moment dallies with the false surmise of the death of the author, a dallying that is outfaced by the scandal of Milton's continued authority, his permanent usurpation of the dialectics of both literary augmentation and authorial resentment. Satan, hardly the old enemy but our old friend, Uncle Satan, incarnates both, since he is still the grandest of all the hero-villains, from Iago and Edmund through Nathanael West's Shrike. Our current literary critical predicament is precisely Uncle Satan's; if one is an experiential literary critic, like my woeful self, one shambles about daily intoning the lines that constitute the poem of our moment and climate:

> And in the lowest deep a lower deep
> Still threatening to devour me opens wide
> To which the hell I suffer seems a heaven.

The times are long gone by in which students of Milton's poetry followed the advice of C. S. Lewis, which was to start the day with a Good Morning's Hatred of Satan. Those were the days of my youth, when professors of literature were a secular clergy. I used to scoff at such a clerisy, but now the mocker is mocked, the biter bitten, and I would as soon be surrounded by a secular clergy as by a pride of displaced social workers. Milton's Satan remains not only the allegory of the post-Enlightenment poet, at her strongest, but of the post-modern critic, at his weakest, "couched with revenge," once the sad transformation atop Mount Niphates is completed. Like our sublime uncle, we fare on from Niphates, where the Tigris, river of Paradise, divides, where Christ is tempted, and from which Adam must contemplate his fallen world. Niphates is Satan's crossing point, after which his fall into dualism is complete, and his heroism forever is dissolved.

Miltonic monism is not a metaphysics but a passion, whether in his fierce youth or in his blind maturity. W. B. C. Watkins stressed what he called Milton's "sensuousness and anthropomorphism," which I would rephrase as "vitalism and theomorphism," each after the mode of J, the strongest writer of the Hebrew Bible, known to Milton as Moses, his truest precursor. Milton revises Homer by transuming him correctively, but he reworks Moses even more cunningly, by a transumption gorgeously expanding the Bible, or displacing it through extraordinary condensation and perspectivizing. J. M. Evans noted that Milton, like the rabbis and fathers before him, had to overcome the interpretive difficulties presented to him not only by the contradictions in Genesis between the Yahwist and the Priestly author, but by what I would term the uncanniness of the Yahwist himself. J's monism (to call it that) is not less than outrageous, but Milton shied away from it only in the representation of God, in his epic's one major aesthetic mistake.

The first true critic of Miltonic monism was W. B. C Watkins, whose Milton was a poet of sensation, perhaps the Milton who most influenced John Keats: "We cannot overstress a fundamental truth about Milton which we find endlessly proliferated in his work. At his most creative, he accepts the whole range from the physical, specifically the senses, to the ultimate Divine as *absolutely unbroken*. This glad acceptance means that he is free to speak of any order of being (extending to inanimate matter) in identical sensuous terms as the great common denominator."

A poet who believes in so much that is transcendent (as Milton did) does not often conceive of the transcendental as being apprehended by our fallen senses. But my language is that of a dualist, as I sadly confess, and Milton poetically could not concede that the senses were fallen, though Christian doctrine surely demands some such concession. We can surmise that all of Milton's heresies fuse in, and issue from, his monism. Anti-Trinitarianism, Mortalism, Arminianism, rejection of *creatio ex nihilo:* these are four versions of a casting out of any dualism except for Jeremiah's espousal of a new inwardness. What may be most normatively Hebraic about Milton is his lack of any sympathy for Saint Paul's version of a Hellenistic dualism. When blindness came upon him, Milton turned even more fervently to the exaltation of all the senses. The celestial light shone inward, in order that the poet might see the invisible, yet see it precisely as if it were visible.

Milton's words are celebrated by his best critics—including Watkins, Christopher Ricks, and William Kerrigan—as being at once physical and moral in their reference, simultaneously acts and cognitions. The Hebrew word behind Saint John's *logos* is *davhar,* as Milton knew, and *davhar* is both a deed and a thought, a word for "word" that does not allow any dualism. Freud does not distinguish between spirit and energy, and neither does Milton. Since Freud proudly confessed himself a dualist, we can infer that the Freudian dualism is akin to Miltonic monism. Each exalts inwardness against things as they outwardly are, and both stances are modes of negation, liberating thought and poetry from a sexual past, while maintaining a considerable repression of memory, regret, desire. The cognitive triumph that ensues is as strong in *Paradise Lost* as it is in *Beyond the Pleasure Principle*.

But is that triumph a liberty, an expression of the human potential for freedom or at least somewhat more freedom than any of us generally possesses? Even if they are akin, are Miltonic monism and Freudian dualism cognitive adventures that quest for human liberty, whether against the satanic and fallen condition or against the aggressive encroachments of the psychic agencies, id and superego, that are respectively below and above the ego?

Northrop Frye, a great Protestant critic of Milton, very much in what can be called Milton's own tradition, tells us that "Liberty for Milton is not something that starts with man: it starts with God. It is something that God is determined he shall have; man cannot want it unless he is in a regenerate state, prepared to accept the inner discipline and responsibility that go with it." I muse upon Frye's observations, and I am certain Milton would have agreed, but I think that the poet in John Milton was too strong not to want liberty, quite naturally, for his own stance and language. The identity of energy and spirit in the unitary Milton constituted his liberty to write his poem. It is another aspect of Miltonic monism that he should have identified his freedom as a poet with Christian liberty, since that identification constitutes his largest heresy, the scope of which encompasses all the others.

If you will not separate spirituality from natural energy, and yet you believe in the Fall of Man, then you necessarily must have a vision of regeneration. Milton's doctrine of regeneration is best expounded by Arthur E. Barker, who emphasizes

how radically Milton's interpretation of the grace of God dif-
fered from characteristic Puritan views. To perfect rather than
abolish the natural man was Milton's quest, despite the blind
poet's contempt for the depravity of his own people, who
had chosen a captain back for Egypt. I wish to suggest that
Miltonic regeneration is more theomorphic than Christian,
unless by Christianity you mean a faith so individual and idiosyncratic that it could be regarded as a sect of one. Milton's
vitalist descendants—Blake, Shelley, Whitman, Lawrence—
were Protestants without being Christians (Blake would have
denied this), yet Milton as poet is more a Miltonist than a
Protestant, and his theomorphic intensity surpasses that of his
descendants, just as it went beyond even Dante's conviction
that he was God's prophet.

Criticism has not yet found an accurate vocabulary for describing precisely how *Paradise Lost* transumes every extra-
poetic belief, including Christianity. What I call transumption
is not just the trope of the interpretive element in poetic allusion, which is what John Hollander takes it to be. Transumption in Milton does not seem to me a trope at all, any more
than his monism seems to me a metaphysical position. I remember arguing almost daily for a long time with my close
friend, the late and much-missed Paul de Man, about his contention that irony was not a trope, but was instead the condition of literary language itself. Transumption may not be the
condition of all belated strong poetry, but it is the poetic
process or essential condition in *Paradise Lost,* and not just the
figure of poetic allusion there. Milton's most characteristic
stance, his *davhar* or word that is also an act and a thought, is
to station himself, with radical originality, in an anxiously
emptied-out present time, between a culturally wealthy but
error-laden past and a weirdly problematic future. Before that
past came a truthful origin, available to us only in and through
Milton's poem. Every account of the past, however beautiful,

is part error, except insofar as it is a commentary upon *Paradise Lost*—though it was written long before Milton's epic. When Milton invokes the Holy Spirit as Muse in Book 1, he asks us implicitly to recall that the Muses originally were the spirits of those springs dedicated to the triumph of Zeus over the titanic gods of the abyss, the old gods, primal and horrible, emblematic of Hades and of death.

Yet the invocation itself never ceases to amaze me by its extraordinary grotesquerie:

> thou from the first
> Wast present, and with mighty wings outspread
> Dove-like sat'st brooding on the vast abyss
> And madest it pregnant . . .

Alastair Fowler, with the authority of his vast learning, says that this is "not a mixed metaphor, but a deliberate allusion to the Hermetic doctrine that God is both masculine and feminine." Nicholas of Cusa is in Fowler's mind, but only Milton is in Milton's mind, as he audaciously asserts his own priority over the Priestly author's account of Creation in Genesis. The Spirit emulates Milton's stance in composing *Paradise Lost*, since the blind bard also broods over the universal blank that, for him, the book of nature has become. By metaleptic reversal, Genesis is transformed into a midrash upon Milton, who himself was present from the first. Milton was there at the earliest, not so much beholding, since the spirit here does not see, but brooding. Neither spirit nor bard is male or female, or male *and* female, since the trope is primarily temporal rather than sexual. To have been present from the first is to have spread out your wings like a dove and to have troped the abyss, caused it to bring forth what was already in it. There is for Milton no abyss of nothingness, but rather a place of being that is already God. Hovering in the Miltonic metalepsis are palpable allusions to Genesis, Luke, and Acts, but also a subtler allusion to Psalm 68, with its promise that though we have lain down among the potsherds, yet shall we be as the wings of a dove. Creation, in Milton's superb first invocation, has become not only the design of his epic, but also the prime trope for his passionate conviction that matter and spirit forever are indistinguishable. Between Milton and God no mediation was necessary, which I again suggest puts Milton's Christianity into question. We need a very different sense of the literal than any now conceptually available to us in order to apprehend the ultimate consequences of Milton's denial of every dualism.

The great dualist in *Paradise Lost* necessarily is Satan, who remains the marvelous scandal of the poem. In Satan, Miltonic transumption has triumphed permanently, so that every subsequent Satan, including the unhappy Tempter in *Paradise Regained,* seems an outdone precursor of the antagonist of *Paradise Lost.* The term "dualism" seems not to have been used before 1700, and perhaps represents the waning of what Neil Forsyth in his study of the Devil calls "the combat myth." *Paradise Lost* is the last and greatest stand of that myth, which had the curious destiny of never receiving a full treatment in canonical Jewish or Christian writings. Shelley charmingly remarked that "The Devil . . . owes everything to Milton," an observation that remains true despite later interventions by Goethe, Dostoyevsky and Thomas Mann. The Devil, as we know, was not a Jewish invention, but goes back at least to the Huwawa of the Sumerians, or the Humbaba of the Assyrians. It is rather a long road from Huwawa, opponent of Gilgamesh, to my personal favorite among literary figures, *Paradise Lost*'s Satan, but there can be no doubt as to Satan's literary ancestry. Between Huwawa and Satan come such formidable charmers as Tiamat, the Babylonian dragon of the sea; Pharaoh in the Exodus narrative; Phaethon in Greece; the fallen star of morning in Isaiah, and the Covering Cherub of Tyre in Ezekiel;

and, perhaps most telling, the Demiurge in the Gnostic scriptures. What all of these lack is Satan's superb personality, the magnificence of his pathos. Speaking only for myself, I have always been in love with the Satan of *Paradise Lost,* and I cannot believe that Milton himself ever started out the day with a neo-Christian Good Morning's Hatred of his own greatest achievement in poetic representation, a hero-villain surpassing even his most direct literary forerunners, Shakespeare's Richard III, Edmund, Iago, and Macbeth. I find in him all my own best qualities, as surely Milton intended, since Satan possesses almost all of Milton's own best qualities, except for monism. Like Milton, Satan is a heroic vitalist, but, unlike Milton, Satan is both the victim and the theorist of a separation between spirit and matter.

Satan of course is a Christian believer, doubtless of the Papist variety, though his belief is more than a little reluctant. What D. P. Walker termed the Decline of Hell, in seventeenth-century discussions of eternal torment, was by no means an un-Miltonic phenomenon, since the Cambridge Platonists, Ralph Cudworth in particular, had profound affinities with Milton's views of regeneration and Christian liberty. Cudworth and Henry More affirmed the eternity of Hell, but rather reluctantly, and essentially tropologically, which was surely Milton's stance. Perhaps Milton's greatest single transumption is his audacious double usurpation of the combat myth, or Satan as the Old Enemy, and what Ronald R. Macdonald invokes as the burial places of memory, the epic underworlds of Virgil and Dante. Making both the combat myth and the burial places of memory altogether his own, Milton partook of what was for him the most crucial priority, the account of catastrophic origins, of the depravity of the elect, of blindness to the light, of the perpetually lower deep within the lowest deep.

William Empson amiably emphasized that "as Satan believes

God to be a usurper he genuinely does believe him to be envious." Milton's God is actually a highly successful usurper, like Milton the poet, and enormously successful usurpations generally cease to be regarded as usurpations, whether in politics, theology, or poetry. Satan is a highly unsuccessful usurper, comparing quite poorly in that one regard to those hero-villains Richard III, Edmund, Iago, and Macbeth. What we cannot forget about Satan in *Paradise Lost* is his earlier rhetoric: heroic, antithetical, dualistic. So compelling is this rhetoric that some complex self-punishment on Milton's part can be surmised. But how could so unitary a being as Milton be self-punishing? If I had to construct a scale with literary self-esteem at one end and aesthetic self-flagellation at the other, then Milton would be at the self-celebratory pole, and Kafka at the extreme of self-punishment. I cannot conceive of John Milton atoning for his own theomorphic intensities, since down to his death a month short of age sixty-six he remained stalwart in his lifelong allegiances. Yet nothing is got for nothing, and the daemons who govern poetry exact their price even from the strongest of poets, be it Milton, the last of the great ancients, or Wordsworth, first and greatest of the moderns. Transuming all your precursors is an extraordinary enterprise, since it is based upon the premise that you can be everything in yourself, at least as a poet. You can be Adam early in the morning, and so you can write what Nietzsche called the primordial poem of mankind. Everything is there for you to name, because you have unnamed it all. Yet Milton was not Emerson or Whitman, who arrived in the American phase of that phenomenon called Enlightenment in its first phase and Romanticism in its second. The Enlightenment tried to break upon Milton, but he thrust it away, into the realm of that grand Cartesian dualist, the heroic Satan.

Let me begin by reminding myself what the best critics in the language have said about the superb and unhappy Satan of

Paradise Lost, whom they have failed to love as he deserves to be loved—but then he is, as I said earlier, the ironic representative or allegory of the post-Miltonic poet at her strongest, and such a poet is dangerous to love, if only because she is the figure of Thanatos as well as Eros, and so her energy fuels the death drive also. Doubtless the death drive is a kind of Jewish joke, perhaps Freud's best joke, another version of my favorite Yiddish apothegm: "Sleep faster; we need the pillows." Satan is neither a Jewish nor a Gentile joke, but rather the strongest representative of the priority of pathos over logos throughout Milton's poetry. The prime fault of most scholarly criticism of Milton is to neglect this priority; here again W. B. C. Watkins is the grand exception, since he affirmed that "passion is always stronger in Milton than reason." Watkins referred to this as "Milton's agonizing ambivalence towards passion," but "ambivalence" seems to me a misleading term in that context. Cognitively, Milton rejected a Calvinist stance toward the separation of nature and grace, and affirmed instead that reason was the mediator which would integrate matter and spirit and thus complete the work of regeneration. Self-esteem, Milton's crucial center, would not permit him ambivalence toward his own passion, which in the dark period of his imprisonment (October through mid-December 1659) must have seemed to him a kind of analogue to the passion of Christ, perhaps his only pragmatic apprehension of the reality of Christ, who bears so little resemblance in Milton to the person presented in the Synoptic Gospels.

A consciousness that declined any separation between spirit and flesh simply refused also to allow a direct opposition between reason and passion. If Satan in *Paradise Lost* is aesthetically superior to God and Messiah, as I think we must acknowledge, it is because passion is grander in him than in them, and Milton overtly accepted the paradox that poetry was more simple, sensuous, and passionate than theology and philosophy. But this hardly means that reason is lacking in Satan, which was the contention of the neoclassical critics of Milton. Addison insisted that amid Satan's impieties "the author has taken care to introduce none that is not big with absurdity, and incapable of shocking a religious reader." More eloquently, Dr. Johnson also dismissed Satan as harmless: "The malignity of Satan foams in haughtiness and obstinacy; but his expressions are commonly general, and not otherwise offensive than as they are wicked." The inadequate heir of Addison and Johnson was C. S. Lewis, for whom Milton's Satan was an absurd egoist, somewhat resembling George Meredith's Sir Willoughby Patterne: "It is a mistake to demand that Satan, any more than Sir Willoughby, should be able to rant and posture through the whole universe without, sooner or later, awaking the comic spirit." The mistake was on the part of the author of *The Screwtape Letters,* since Satan did not seem comic to John Milton. Hazlitt wisely noted of Satan that "His strength of mind was matchless as his strength of body" and "His power of action and of suffering was equal . . . He was baffled, not confounded." Let us follow Hazlitt by surveying, as closely as possible, the separation of powers in Satan, the dualism into which he has been thrown.

I would hesitate to describe any single speech by Satan as his grandest, except for his soliloquy upon Mount Niphates, at the start of Book 4. Yet it is difficult to admire too much his marvelous opening address to Beelzebub, as they float side by side upon the burning lake. In this speech, as always, there is a preponderance of pathos over logos, yet the pathos is dialectical, being antithetical to most human passion. Satan's despair is the despair of having been thrown, outward and downward, from the realms of light to the darkness visible of Hell. This is a Virgilian pathos, and begins with an allusion to Aeneas' reaction when he sees a manifestation of Hector's ghost even as Troy falls: "ei mihi, qualis erat! quantum mutatus ab illo / Hectore." Beelzebub is no longer a Hector, which means that Satan himself is no longer an Achilles. But how much still abides, because he remains more than half a god, however fallen. Not much trace survives in him of the Satan of the Hebrew Bible; he is no accuser, no servant of the heavenly court. He is a great vitalist horribly disfigured, but not in his will:

> What though the field be lost?
> All is not lost; the unconquerable will,
> And study of revenge, immortal hate,
> And courage never to submit or yield:
> And what is else not to be overcome?

Fowler notes the allusion to Edward Fairfax's Spenserian translation (1600) of Tasso's *Jerusalem Delivered,* in which Satan addresses "his fiends and sprites":

> Oh! be not then the courage perish'd clean
>   That whilome dwelt within your haughty thought,
> When, arm'd with shining fire and weapons keen,
>   Against the angels of proud heav'n we fought:
> I grant we fell on the Phlegrean green,
>   Yet good our cause was, though our fortune naught;
> For chance assisteth oft th'ignobler part,
> We lost the field, yet lost we not our heart.

Between the Tasso-Fairfax Satan and the Miltonic Satan there intervenes the gigantic context of the Longinian or agonistic sublime, with its Pindaric colorings. "We lost the field, yet lost we not our heart" knows little of the will's revenge against time and time's "It was." The Nietzschean courage of *Paradise Lost*'s Satan may be a lie, but as such it is a heroic fiction, a lying against time, a surge that is itself a poem, the fiction of duration. When we hear the rhetorical question—

"And what is else not to be overcome?"—we knowingly hear the poetic voice proper, the image of voice materializing itself in and by the will. We hear it again in the most profound allegory of poetic origins ever given to us, when Satan in Book 5 replies to Milton's own surrogate, the angel Abdiel, severe flame of zeal, who has admonished Satan that Christ was the Father's agent in the Creation:

> who saw
> When this creation was? Remember'st thou
> Thy making, while the maker gave thee being?
> We know no time when we were not as now;
> Know none before us, self-begot, self-raised
> By our own quickening power . . .

To cite Augustine against Satan here, as C. S. Lewis did, seems to me both redundant and misplaced; it is rather like quoting Augustine against Emerson's "Self-Reliance" or against Walt Whitman or Pater or Nietzsche. Milton overtly assigns to Satan a Gnostic stance, one which sees God and Christ as mere versions of the Demiurge. That is sound Christian doctrine, but the rhetoric of Satan, his strength of pathos here, is quite another matter. Does Milton, as a strong poet, as the very archetype of the modern strong poet, ever allow himself to know poetically a time when he was not as now? Does he know any poet *before* him, even Moses, or the Jesus of the Gospel parables? Is he not, in his own regard, self-begotten as a poet, despite his great original, Spenser, and the hero-villains brought to perfection by Shakespeare? Is not the poet of *Paradise Lost* represented as being self-raised by his own quickening power? I do not mean the poet as the man John Milton, but rather John Milton, the poet as poet. When Augustine (in *City of God*) denounces the Manichaeans for not recognizing that their souls were not a part of God, nor of the same nature as

God, but were created by God to be far different from their Creator, would Milton have been as ready to agree if Augustine had been denouncing all poets as such? The acute Augustinian dualism is simply not Miltonic, and when Satan ironically affirms that dualism by denying its consequences, then we ought to be very wary of assimilating Milton to Augustine, as Lewis automatically did.

I have said that to speak of Milton's monism or of his own heroic vitalism is a poor way of speaking, yet still they remain all we have as starting points when we seek to apprehend the deepest paradoxes of *Paradise Lost*. That the poem is Protestant is palpable, yet it is neither Augustinian nor Calvinist, since it teaches that the will can be made free again, can be regenerated or restored so that our former Edenic liberty can return within this life. The fallen Adam need not be altogether dependent upon God's will, and since the Spirit does not make particular and absolute choices, as it does in Calvin, a general and conditional election is made available to more than just the saints. There is for Milton a path between Satan and Augustine, but this path is for Milton the man. Is there a poet's path, a way for the poet as poet, that can be clearly divided from the satanic predicament? Since Satan is not just an astonishing poetic achievement, but in a clear sense is the achievement of poetry itself, how does Milton represent his own freedom from Satan, insofar as he enjoys such a freedom? The issue is not being a true poet and so being of the devil's party without knowing it, but rather that Satan is a true enough poet to be of Milton's sect without knowing it, despite the satanic rejection of Abdiel's admonitions. Shelley, as I've noted, told us that the Devil owed everything to Milton, and that is the center of the paradox. Christ, after all, is a poetic disaster in *Paradise Lost;* we remember him riding in the Chariot of Paternal Deity, leading an armored attack upon the hapless hoplites of Satan's legions. Aesthetically that is not acceptable, while spiritually it is horrible, unless you are very fond of tank warfare.

Poetic representation has great difficulties with any monistic vision, though the account of the Creation in Book 7 is the most successful depiction of the coming into being of a monistic world that I have read. Milton's God, alas, is a catastrophe rather than a catastrophe creation, but not because of Milton's monism. Dante showed Milton a better way, which Milton declined to take. I cannot explain the disaster of Milton's God, who resembles, say, Ronald Reagan more than he does, say, Sigmund Freud—who always appears in my own dreams as Yahweh the Father, complete with cigars and Edwardian three-piece suit. Milton after all was most unsympathetic to earthly tyrants, and he is not very persuasive when he moves the divine right of kings back up into the remote heavens, with time-serving angels circling the throne while chanting praises of their irascible and self-righteous monarch.

The paradox of Milton's Protestant denial of dualism has been explored by William Kerrigan, as a Freudian problem in psychogenesis, and by John Guillory, as an issue in poetic authority. I do not think that we can ever answer the question of what is the authority that prior poetry possesses over or for any poetry that wants to call itself "modern," from Callimachus in Alexandria down to our moment. Authority demands obedience, and strong poets are never obedient, John Milton least of all. Plato may have taught Milton that a dependence upon divine laws rather than upon men brought liberty, but Milton's sense of poetic freedom does not seem to me at all Platonic. Milton was not interested in an authority that drew its strength from the past. Power, for Milton, resided in the pathos of the present, and in *potentia,* the likely pathos of the future. What Hannah Arendt termed "the Roman pathos for foundation" is alien to *Paradise Lost*. Augmenting the foundation is a satanic enterprise in the poem; such an enterprise builds up Pandemonium, or Saint Peter's, hardly suitable for the spirit that prefers before all temples the pure and upright heart of the sect of one—Abdiel or Milton, solitary warrior or isolated blind bard, guardians of the truth that obeys a highly individual inner light.

Hazlitt remains Milton's best critic, despite Dr. Johnson's acute insight, which established our contemporary understanding of the workings of transumption or Miltonic allusiveness. In remarking that Milton alone could maintain his originality while remolding all his precursors, Hazlitt touched upon the Miltonic refusal of belatedness, and shows us that belatedness and dualism were not two forms of the same evil for the poet of *Paradise Lost*. To be first or earliest was also to fuse flesh and spirit; to lurk behind, like Satan, was to have dissociated sensuousness and consciousness, and so to have become a peeping Tom. Casting out dualism, Milton became the absolute master of its representation, with the Satan of Books 1 through 4 as his masterpiece in what I suppose must be called the Augustinian mode, a mode, however, transmogrified by Milton to purposes utterly distinct from Augustine's own priorities. Abolishing the natural man, yielding up the earthly city, encountering truth through an antithetical dialectic of clashing faiths: these are not Miltonic procedures. Augustine enshrined dualism; Milton portrayed it only that he might defeat it.

But the pathos of Satan, though it is not Milton's own pathos, has a power in *Paradise Lost* that Milton himself indubitably underestimated, perhaps because dualism was not for him a temptation. We love Satan not because we too are necessarily rebellious but for the same reason we secretly love his precursor Macbeth: both hero-villains are terribly interesting to us because of their terrible inwardness. In them we find the self-obsessiveness that always makes us more interesting to ourselves than anyone else can be except for those brief periods of what Freud calls overestimations of the object, or being in love. And if there is Macbeth in Satan, as well as Edmund and Iago, there is something of Hamlet as well. Like Hamlet, Satan does not need us, except as an audience for his tragedy. Hamlet does not even want us, except to pack his theater of mind, while Satan does want us, since he does have a moderate interest in populating Hell. It seems perverse of me to suggest that Satan fills more of an empty space in our hearts than he did for Milton, but few among us, if any, quite share in Milton's strong ego, in his healthy and justified self-esteem.

Satan does not leave us surprised by sin; rather, we are surprised by Satan, because he is as uncanny as the Yahwist's Yahweh, or as Shakespeare's Edmund. Satan is quicker than we are, and always exceeds us in quickening power. Alas, being an excellent Augustinian dualist, Satan also quickens the death drive in us, and perhaps even incarnates the Freudian chiasmus that constitutes the relation between Eros and the death drive. Freud always feared the destruction of his own dualism by the force of aggressivity, as enshrined in the Adlerian heresy that infuriated our father Freud even more than did the deviations of Jung, Rank, Reich, and all the other heresiarchs. We fear that force also, and so we fear Satan, even as we feel his attractiveness, but Milton is not as vulnerable to the temptations of Satan, or to his threats. His stance toward his own creature, Satan, lacks the amiable intimacy that Marlowe displays in regard to Mephistopheles, Barabas, and even Tamburlaine. Something of Shakespeare's stance in regard to Iago or Macbeth has found its way into Milton's conceptual rhetoric, which may be why *Paradise Lost* seems more a tragic drama than an epic whenever Satan is the focus of our concern.

Satan's is a tragedy neither of blood nor of mind, despite his overt resemblances to Macbeth and his subtler affinities with Hamlet. *Paradise Lost* after all is not Satan's tragedy, any more than *King Lear* is Edmund's or *Othello* is Iago's. It is our tragedy, because we are Adam and Eve; if Satan himself is tragic, then his tragedy is what he wanted it to be, a tragedy of fate— though in the Freudian sense, which is also pre-Socratic, in which character is fate. Ethos is the *daimon* in Satan, even though pathos is his glory, his abiding strength. I return to him atop Mount Niphates because that is his farewell to glory, and the start of his progressive degradation by the ungrateful Milton. Also, its ten opening lines, according to Edward Phillips, are the earliest passage composed in the poem, intended as the beginning of a tragic drama on the Fall. When Satan expresses remorse, we are very moved, but we become dubious when he goes on to murmur Ciceronian reflections upon the true nature of indebtedness:

> and in a moment quit
> The debt immense of endless gratitude,
> So burdensome still paying, still to owe;
> Forgetful what from him I still received,
> And understood not that a grateful mind
> By owing owes not, but still pays at once
> Indebted and discharged; what burden then?

I do not find myself persuaded by this, and wonder when Milton himself ever showed such handsome gratitude toward any forerunner poets. Far more splendid is Satan's grand rhetorical recovery at the close of this address of despair:

> So farewell hope, and with hope farewell fear,
> Farewell remorse: all good to me is lost;
> Evil be thou my good . . .

This immeasurably self-conscious dualism fulfills a prophecy of Isaiah, and mounts to a new pinnacle in the mode of Macbeth. C. S. Lewis descended to a lower deep in translating this as "Nonsense be thou my sense," if only because Satan, like

Macbeth at his close, is never more cogent than here. Casting out remorse, as in Satan's descendants Shelley, Nietzsche, and Yeats, is a repudiation of what Shelley called the dark idolatry of self. Nietzsche urged us to take the final step and have the grace to forgive ourselves, after which the whole drama of fall and redemption would be worked through within each of us. Satan, never less self-deceived, here makes himself prior to his transumed source in Isaiah, while also thwarting Shelley's attempt to transume Milton, or the Nietzschean and Yeatsian tropings upon Shelley. We are shown by Satan that self-forgiveness is not possible, because the farewell to remorse must involve also a farewell to the good. Moral idiocy, contra Lewis, is scarcely the issue; the cost of confirmation is, when fear must be part of the good. In choosing dualism, and then a single polarity within the dyad, Satan chooses to be himself at the highest possible price. His domain will grow, yet his ethos must decline, as he knows, precisely and with despair. He knows also that this is both his best and his worst moment, and that pragmatically the best and the worst will never be untangled for him again.

Can we ever resolve the moral puzzle that Satan's aesthetic success constitutes? Our best clue, as I have been hinting, is that Milton could not share in our puzzlement. I cannot believe that history accounts for this difference between Milton and ourselves, or that any historicism, old or new, will lighten this darkness. The freedom of the saints, or Christian liberty from the Laws of Moses, meant a great deal to Milton, but less, early and late, than did his peculiar vocation as a poet, conceived by him as a prophetic calling. John Guillory, in a fine sentence, reminds us that "The failed prophet in *Paradise Lost* is called Satan, and he is . . . a successful poet." In *Paradise Lost*, I would agree, tropological triumph accompanies literal defeat, while the victory of Messiah, God's son, is a figurative botch. Sacred and secular, to Milton, constituted only another unnecessary dualism.

Paradise Lost is the most resolutely archaic of literary works, more archaic even than Hesiod, or Genesis, or Freud's *Totem and Taboo*. This archaic insistence underlies, I suspect, Milton's ultimate refusal of the greatest gift Shakespeare could have given him, the representation of inner change by showing characters pondering their own utterances. Satan does not develop, and is never modified by listening to himself, as are Edmund, Iago, Macbeth, and Hamlet above all. When Satan addresses himself, he either confirms the major change of his Fall or defies it, but he does not learn to change further. Endlessly agonistic, he never ceases to ask himself the triple question of the sublime mode: Am I more than, equal to, or less than I was—or, rather, than others still are? He knows that it does not matter what he answers. He is the perpetual poem of his climate, an angel upon whom the sun has gone down, a relic of having been thrown out of heaven by Messiah, and so he is the true form of loss.

Why did Milton invest so heavily in Satan, rather than in God or in Messiah? Any formalist can answer this question easily enough by discoursing upon Satan's narrative function, first in Christian myth, then in *Paradise Lost*. But Satan is vastly in excess of his utility in the narrative of Milton's epic. Scholars go on telling us that Satan is there for the myth, and for the poem, yet the reader's sublime always replies that the poem is there for Satan. It is Milton's Satan that we must think upon when the Western literary sublime demands to be exemplified and defined. To hate the Satan of *Paradise Lost,* to find him foolish or inadequate, is simply to fail to have been found by him. The best editor of *Paradise Lost* to this date is the learned and ingenious Alastair Fowler, who tells us that "Milton's God is surprising enough to be a universal father fig-

ure; enigmatic enough to be the subject of interminable scho-
lastic debates; sublime enough to be awe-inspiring; remote
enough from our wishes to be partly true." What is being described there is Fowler's God, and not Milton's ill-tempered,
sanctimonious bore. Let me transpose Fowler: Milton's Satan
is surprising enough to be a universal prodigal son; puzzling
enough to force criticism beyond its limits; sublime enough to
usurp the sublime forever; near enough to our desires to be
wholly true, when our desires flower in the phantasmagoria of
nightmare.

Milton's major desire was to assert his own identity as poet-
prophet, far surpassing Moses and Isaiah and the authors of
the New Testament. *Paradise Lost* rather alarmingly begins true
time with God's proclamation that Christ is his only begotten
son, an announcement that shocks Satan into rebellion. How
would Milton have reacted if his contemporaries had included
a divine poet stronger than himself, say a Shakespeare devoted
to composing the national religious epic? Satan, until the
nasty surprise of learning that he owes his very existence to
Christ, had been the glorious Lucifer, foremost among God's
loyal flatterers. Down he comes, upon ceasing to be his father's
favorite, and as he starts downward and outward he declares
that he has fathered himself. To have Spenser as one's original
a safe century back is one thing; to have had an older contemporary Spenser or a Shakespeare would have been quite another. Modern scholars keep telling me how pious Milton was,
but I do not doubt that Milton in Satan's position would have
done precisely what he has his Satan do, and would have ex-
claimed, even more fiercely than Satan: "I know no time when
I was not as now; I know none before me."

The secret links between Milton the poet and Satan the poet
have been uncovered by Kerrigan, Riggs, Guillory, and others,
all following in the wide wake of Samuel Taylor Coleridge, but
I do not endorse their conclusion that Milton's implicit com-

parison of his epic quest to Satan's is made in order to explore the dangers, moral and aesthetic, that the blind poet courts in composing *Paradise Lost*. That is to come a touch short of Milton's egotistical sublime, which finds a freedom of figuration only when it tropes two matters in the poem: the satanic predicament and the work of Creation. The rhetoric of *Paradise Lost*, like that of Blake, Whitman, and Hart Crane after it, is a rhetoric of desire, a desire for more life, and for the simple, sensuous and passionate exercise of poetry. Milton creates not out of nothing but out of his own unitary self, toward which he manifests no ambivalences. Satan of course creates poor Satan, not out of Lucifer or the unitary self but out of the abyss or nothing. If Shakespeare was, as Harold Goddard insisted, an unfallen Hamlet, then Milton was, I would insist, an unfallen Satan, a Lucifer, and has the same relationship to his own Satan that Shakespeare may have had to Hamlet. The true relation between Milton and his prodigal creation, Satan, is precisely that: Satan is the fallen form of John Milton, who lived and died a Lucifer, and is still the morning and evening star of the poetry in our language.

V

ENLIGHTENMENT
AND
ROMANTICISM

O UR CLASSICAL definition of what the literary sublime asserts can be found in the opening sentences of Thomas Weiskel's *The Romantic Sublime* (1976):

> The essential claim of the sublime is that man can, in feeling and in speech, transcend the human. What, if anything, lies beyond the human—God or the gods, the daemon or Nature—is matter for great disagreement. What, if anything, defines the range of the human is scarcely less sure.

A few sentences further on, Weiskel concludes his book's first paragraph with the fine apothegm: "A humanistic sublime is an oxymoron." Weiskel's power as a theorist of the sublime is condensed in his implication that the Hebraic or Christian sublime, the Homeric sublime, the daemonic sublime, the natural sublime—all evade oxymoronic status. They may also evade precise definition, indeed may blend into one another, but none of them is so problematical and paradoxical as that seeming self-contradiction, a humanistic sublime. Sublime poets who are crucially humanistic in some aspects—Milton, Blake, Wordsworth, Shelley, Keats, Whitman, Stevens— must forsake the sublime when they foreground humanistic concerns.

Weiskel, as a critic, ultimately was in the tradition of Longinus rather than Aristotle, which is to say that Weiskel was not a formalist but was himself a sublime critic. Transcendence of the human in speech, particularly in the utterance within a tradition of utterance that is poetry, necessarily relies upon the trope of hyperbole, an overthrowing (or overtaking, or over-reaching) that is closer to simplification through intensity than it is to exaggeration. Transcendence of the human in feeling is a universal experience (or illusion) and itself transcends most modes of utterance. Shakespeare is peculiarly triumphant at representing the sublime of feeling, as in Cleopatra's magnificent lament for Antony:

> The crown o' th' earth doth melt. My lord!
> O, wither'd is the garland of the war,
> The soldier's pole is fall'n! Young boys and girls
> Are level now with men; the odds is gone,
> And there is nothing left remarkable
> Beneath the visiting moon.

The soldier's pole serves as the standard of measurement, and since it is fallen, all distinction, all difference ("the odds") is gone. Cleopatra deftly cries out that the sublime is gone with her Antony while marvelously speaking in sublime accents, which tells us that she is all of the sublime that is left. What determines the presence or absence of the sublime is the standard of measurement, consisting initially in the Platonic ideas, but later honed down by Plato to a pragmatic knowledge able to answer the questions: more? equal to? less than? I am following Hannah Arendt's Heideggerian reading of *The Republic* in her essay on authority in *Between Past and Future*. Cleopatra sublimely elegizes the passing of the sublime, because everything that remains is less than the lost Antony. What Cleopatra knows is that the sublime is agonistic, a knowledge crucial to theorists of the sublime from Longinus to Weiskel.

Angus Fletcher, who seems to me Weiskel's authentic precursor in my generation of critics, emphasized in his seminal book *Allegory* (1964) that "the sublime appears to provide a cosmology for the poet." Taking as his own the Longinian desire to free us from the slavery of pleasure, or of a mere dullness, Fletcher followed Shelley's Longinian *Defence of Poetry* in emphasizing that the function of the sublime was to work, by "difficult ornament" and by heightened ambivalences, so as to make us share in its agon, its ceaseless struggle against the superficial. Weiskel's *The Romantic Sublime*, like Fletcher's *Allegory*, shares the deep design upon us of Longinus and Shelley. We are to be persuaded to yield up easier pleasures for more difficult pleasures, or as Weiskel phrases this, we are to move from the egotistical sublime to the negative sublime:

> The egotistical sublime culminates in an intense ambivalence. Memory and desire practice a cheat: they lead us to a bosom all right, but the cost of the regression and the solitude or desertion implicit in its object have made that object a hated thing. In terms of what Freud called the family romance, identity is regarded with all the unresolved ambivalence of an Oedipal crisis in which there is, strangely, no symbolic father to come to the rescue. Yet we cannot fail to note that the structure of the egotistical sublime ends precisely at the point of ambivalence in which we found the beginnings of the negative sublime.

All theorists of the sublime confront certain masterpieces of emotional ambivalence: the Oedipal struggle, the taboo, transference are among them. Equal and opposed feelings, antithetical forces that are enemy brothers or sisters, appear to be the emotive basis for the sublime. Yet ambivalence increased to excess becomes irony, which destroys the sublime. Acutely aware of this danger, Weiskel chose to defend against it through the example of Wallace Stevens, who in one of his aspects or perpetual phases is a last strong version of the egotistical sublime of Wordsworth and of Walt Whitman. As a regressive structure, Stevens's sublime refuses to grow up, but what does growing up mean in and for a poem anyway, except the loss of power? Weiskel, as a sublime critic rather than a mere moralist, made his own allegiance movingly clear: "Poets, however, are up to such risks, which in any case they have no choice about.

It is not in the assumption of spiritual risks that the egotistical romantic pays for the hybris of his sublimation. Nothing is got for nothing. The cost is there, and it is paid in the text, not in extrinsic circumstance."

Neil Hertz, working in the deconstructive mode of Paul de Man's conceptual rhetoric, and influenced also by French feminist revisions of Freud, in *The End of the Line* credited Weiskel for dwelling intensely on the anxieties of the pre-Oedipal or maternal sublime, and yet criticized him for "the relief he seemed to have experienced as an interpreter in at last bringing it all home to the Father." Hertz, I think, chooses to forget that the sublime takes place *between* origin and aim or end, and that the only Western trope that avoids both origin and end is the trope of the Father, which is only to say that we do not speak of "Father Nature." Weiskel indeed is closer to Freud than Lacan or Derrida are, because he does not read his Freud through Heidegger.

Throughout *The Romantic Sublime*, Weiskel works toward a difficult kind of literary criticism, at once moral or primary and de-idealizing or antithetical. This may not be possible to attain; certainly I, for one, have failed to achieve it. In Wordsworth criticism, it would reconcile Matthew Arnold and A. C. Bradley, M. H. Abrams and Geoffrey Hartman. Perhaps Wordsworth as poet of nature and as poet of the sublime can accommodate such divergent critics, but they necessarily must fail to accommodate one another. But Weiskel's attempt is itself sublime; it involves yielding up easier pleasures for more severe pleasures, and perhaps it will mark always one of the limits of twentieth-century criticism of the High Romantic poets. Immensely moved as I am by all of Weiskel's study, I am most touched to meditation by his bold effort to define the Wordsworthian imagination:

> What then is this "awful Power" which Wordsworth names "Imagination"? In the late version [of *The Prelude*], Wordsworth will tell us that the power is "so called/Through sad incompe-

tence of human speech" (6.592–593), but the name is of course entirely right, for the power of sight does rise in intensity from memory through salience to the occlusion of the visible. The Imagination may be structurally defined as a power of resistance to the Word, and in this sense it coincides exactly with the psychological necessity of originality. But a structural definition merely locates an experience; as an experience or moment the Imagination is an extreme consciousness of self mounting in dialectical recoil from the extinguishing of the self which an imminent identification with the symbolic order enjoins. Hence the Imagination rises "Like an unfather'd vapour": it is at once the ego's need and its attempt to be *unfathered*, to originate itself and thereby refuse acknowledgment to a superior power. The imagination is not an evasion of the oedipus complex but a rejection of it. From a certain perspective (such perspective, for example, as is implied by the history of poetic influence) that rejection is purely illusory, a fiction. To reject the oedipus complex is not, after all, to dispel it. But the fiction is a necessary and saving one; it founds the self and secures the possibility—the chance for a self-conviction—of originality. And so Wordsworth can turn to his "conscious soul" (1850) and say, "I recognise thy glory."

A necessary and saving fiction is both a Stevensian trope and a return to Weiskel's own yearning to establish a structure and a psychology for transcendence. The hope, as in Emerson and in Stevens, is a very American modification of the European Protestant ethos, and Weiskel takes his rightful place in that tradition, both choosing and being chosen by it. The tradition had been modified before, by the European Enlightenment, through a transformation, really a saving reduction, of transcendence into that mode termed either sensibility or the sentimental.

The sentimental, neither as a Victorian exaltation of middle-class morality nor as a modern celebration of proletarian, natural simplicity, is a crucial mode of thought and feeling in the middle and later eighteenth century. Martin Price, one of its foremost expositors, calls it "a vehement, often defiant assertion of the value of man's feelings." This self-conscious, overtly dramatic manifestation, sincere despite its theatrical overtones, was taken as the demonstration of a receptive spirit, compassionate and humane, and then was named as "sensibility." Its great exemplar was Rousseau, and its principal British representative was the uncanny novelist Laurence Sterne.

In a complex fusion, the passion for the sublime mode, agonistic and transcendental, was able to reconcile itself with the milder responsiveness of sensibility. This fusion informs the poets Young, Thomson, Gray, Collins, Smart, and Cowper, and appears also in the archaic impostures of Macpherson as Ossian and Chatterton as Rowley. In Robert Burns and the early Blake, the unstable union of sensibility and the sublime helped stimulate the only poets of the eighteenth century who could rival Dryden and Pope. The aura of the poets of sensibility and the sublime has pervaded Anglo-American poetry ever since, partly through its Romantic descendants, and partly because of a curious modernity that we apprehend in the perilous balance and frequently catastrophic fates of these doom-eager poets. William Cowper's magnificent lyric "The Castaway" ends with the perfect motto for the poetry of sensibility and the sublime, a borderline poetry that fears, yet courts madness:

> No voice divine the storm allayed,
>   No light propitious shone,
> When, snatched from all effectual aid,
>   We perished, each alone:
> But I beneath a rougher sea,
> And whelmed in deeper gulfs than he.

Blake, who neither feared nor coveted madness, returned from sensibility to transcendence, but at a cost we seem unwilling to comprehend.

❧

As a heroic vitalist, Blake casts out all dualisms; as an apocalyptic visionary, he seems in certain respects a kind of Gnostic, and Gnosticism is the most dualistic mode of belief ever advocated in Western tradition. Northrop Frye's Blake imaginatively transcends the cloven fiction presented by a simultaneous monism and dualism, and indeed escapes the consequences of innumerable contradictions in stance and argument via the same procedure, almost as though Blake were Hegel, but crucified upside down, as it were. *Fearful Symmetry,* in my judgment, remains Frye's best work, rather than *Anatomy of Criticism* or *The Great Code,* but as a commentary upon Blake it seems to me a beautiful idealization in which I can no longer share. Only two books truly mattered to Blake, as Frye noted: the Bible and Milton. Blake's Bible is indistinguishable from Frye's Blakean *Great Code,* and I now repudiate my youthful efforts to Judaize William Blake in a book called *Blake's Apocalypse* and in an earlier work *The Visionary Company.* The Hebrew Bible is canceled, not fulfilled, in the Christian mythology of Blake and of Frye. And just so, Milton also is canceled rather than fulfilled in Blake's *Milton: A Poem in Two Books.* That is the normal procedure of strong poets, and criticism serves us ill when it idealizes the relationship between the Bible and Blake, or the Bible and Milton. The figure of Milton in Blake is just that, a trope, a figurative attempt at transumption, and I would say now a failed attempt, though a beautiful failure.

If you are a monist, particularly a kind of heroic vitalist, then you require a psychology of the will rather than a depth psychology of the sort that goes from Plato through Montaigne to culminate at last in Sigmund Freud. Depth psychology is a dualistic mode, consonant with a dualistic rhetoric and a dualistic cosmology. We ought never to forget that psychology, rhetoric, and cosmology are three names for a single entity. Blake is confusing, and ultimately richly confused, because his personal psychology is always dualistic, despite his desires, while his rhetoric and his cosmology manifest a wavering split between monistic and dualistic visions. More simply, Blake rejects nature and the natural man, in a vehemently Gnostic manner, while simultaneously he affirms the oxymoronic stance of what I once termed an apocalyptic humanism. I would not call it that any more, and I find myself wishing that Blake had been able to see that he lacked a true psychology of the poetic will, despite his ceaseless attempts to mythologize such a psychology. The Nietzschean will to revenge against time, and against time's "It was," is Blake's will also, but he deceived himself into a very different view. Although his prophecy was negative and apocalyptic, he misrepresented it as the stance of Isaiah and Milton, neither of whom would abandon history to the Accuser.

Blake etched the plates of his brief epic *Milton* in 1809 and 1810, but the poem seems to have been written from 1800 to 1803, though substantially revised until it was engraved. That makes it almost contemporary with Wordsworth's two-part *Prelude* of 1799, its principal rival as a High Romantic transumption of Miltonic epic. Like *Paradise Regained*, Blake's work had as its thematic model the Book of Job; Blake's audacious originality comes in his representation of John Milton as epic hero. Like the 1799 *Prelude*, Blake's *Milton* can be regarded as an extended crisis lyric, since an internalization of the agonistic sublime is crucial to both poems, with John Milton serving as fathering force and as the agonistic other. I remember writing once that Blake's audacity is nowhere emulated in modern poetry, which does not give us such works as, say, *Browning: A Poem in Two Books* by Ezra Pound, or *Eliot Agonistes* by Robert Lowell. I would be delighted to read a brief epic entirely centered upon Auden or Stevens by James Merrill, or a sustained dramatic monologue spoken by Whitman or Stevens, as composed by John Ashbery. Merrill has flirted with such a mode in parts of *The Changing Light at Sandover*, while Ashbery spookily verges upon such moments in *Litany* and *A Wave*. Blake remains unique among the strongest post-Enlightenment poets in having worked through many of the implications of such a venture.

I want to speculate more fully upon one of those implications. Can you "correct" a precursor poet without savagely caricaturing him? Is there really a sense in which one strong poem can fulfill or complete a poem of the same eminence by another poet who comes earlier? I do not know of a more central question than this in the entire vexed area of poetry and belief, because an answer, if we could find one, might define forever what Andrew Marvell in his poem on *Paradise Lost* calls "misdoubting" the intent of Milton's argument, a misdoubting leading to the supposed fear "That he would ruin (for I saw him strong)/The sacred Truths to Fable and Old Song."

All strong poets, whether Dante or Milton or Blake, must ruin the sacred truths to fable and old song, precisely because the essential condition for poetic strength is that the new song, one's own, always must be a song of one's self, whether it be called the *Divine Comedy,* or *Paradise Lost,* or *Milton: A Poem in Two Books.* Every sacred truth not one's own becomes a fable, an old song that requires corrective revision. Dante completes and fulfills Virgil; Milton transumes everybody, including the Yahwist; and Blake so rewrites Milton and the Bible as to make them commentaries upon his own Bible of Hell. Once I thought that such sublime caricatures of precursors were the products of a kind of poetic repression, since repression is after all a mode of idealization—though Freud insisted on this matter the other way around, with repression always taking priority, so that every idealization was dependent upon repression.

But there are other drives in us besides Eros and Thanatos, which I think is why we long for poetry, whether we know it or not. There is also the will that one's name not be scattered, to adopt the language of the J writer. The will of the strong poet is not identical either with the will to live or with the will to die. Poetic immortality is not a trope for the fear of death or for the blessing of more life, and once at least Freud admitted something like this. I am not implying that the poetic drive ought to have the same cognitive status in Freud as Eros and Thanatos. Rather, the poetic will to immortality, or lust for priority, shows that the two Freudian drives are themselves defensive tropes, or what Freud called superstitions. Freud thought that the ambition for immortality was another superstition, but it seems to me it is more primal than that and takes priority over belief of any kind. In Freud's view, only a small elect among us were not obsessed neurotics, repressing murderous impulses against our loved ones. A mere handful could free their thinking from its sexual past, and thus achieve the higher superstition of Freud himself, who asserted that "My own superstition has its roots in suppressed ambition (immortality) and in my case takes the place of that anxiety about death which springs from the normal uncertainty of life."

That Freudian sentence would be a superb commentary upon Milton's *Lycidas*, or upon Blake's *Milton*. Blake idealizes his ambition more than Milton does in *Lycidas* and in the invocations of *Paradise Lost*, and rather more than Freud does. The imaginative drive or poetic will of Blake's *Milton* is essentially autobiographical, in that Blake represents himself as his own Job, overcoming a purely personal Satan by following the example not of the historical Milton but of his own Milton, which is to say his own sense of the poetic calling. Blake's Milton rises up from the heaven of his own vision, where he finds himself unhappy, and resolves to descend. He is quite bored with an unimaginative heaven where he has nothing whatsoever to do except walk around "pondering the intricate mazes of Providence" in a nasty Blakean parody of the Fallen Angels in *Paradise Lost*. Therefore, Blake's Milton "took off the robe of the promise, & ungirded himself from the oath of God," becoming an antinomian, and yielding up all Calvinism once for all. "To claim the Hells, my Furnaces," this Milton says, "I go to Eternal Death," which means that, like Christopher Smart in *Jubilate Agno,* this bard will see "the furnace come up at last" in our generative life, unkindly called an eternal death by the weeping assembly that Milton abandons behind him in the heavens. Milton's descent through the shadow of the cycles of history looks like the fall of his own Satan, a comet or star going outward and downward. Blake gazes upward and tells us what he sees, or wants to see:

Then first I saw him in the Zenith as a falling star
Descending perpendicular, swift as the swallow or swift
And on my left foot falling on the tarsus, entered there;
But from my left foot a black cloud redounding spread over
   Europe . . .

Earliest, Milton was Blake's Lucifer, an unfallen Satan but in the act of descent, since the precursor must be falling if the belated bard is to experience in himself the incarnation of the poetic character. The tarsus (the bone he lands on) plays upon Saul of Tarsus, struck down by a great light upon the road to Damascus, even as Blake is struck here by the quick, perpendicular illumination of the truth of Milton's fall into our universe of death. Foster Damon equated that redounding black cloud spread over Europe with Puritanism, but it is more precisely the shadow of Milton, or the Miltonic influence upon poets coming after him. Blake wants the illumination rather than the shadow, so that his ankle, trope of poetic stance, will be emblematic of poetic transformation, Saul into Paul. So, in a revision of his own trope, Blake then ventures an audacious identification with Milton, as though the two truly could become a single poet:

But Milton entering my Foot; I saw in the nether
Regions of the Imagination; also all men on Earth,
And all in Heaven, saw in the nether regions of the
    Imagination
In Ulro beneath Beulah, the vast breach of Miltons descent.
But I knew not that it was Milton, for man cannot know
What passes in his members till periods of Space & Time
Reveal the secrets of Eternity: for more extensive
Than any other earthly things, are Mans earthly lineaments.
And all this Vegetable World appeared on my left Foot,
As a bright sandal formd immortal of precious stones & gold:
I stooped down & bound it on to walk forward thru' Eternity.

I interpret this both as a stunning tribute to Milton's monistic vision and its saving influence upon Blake and his poetry,
and also as an involuntary self-revelation on the part of Blake
the poet, a confession of his inability to achieve the heroic vitalism of his theomorphic precursor. What Blake generally
terms with disdain "this Vegetable World" now appears on his
foot as a sandal made of "precious stones & gold." This redeemed or monistic vision of nature ensues from "Milton entering my Foot," even though Blake is careful to assert that his
own poetic will must choose to accept the gift: "I stooped
down & bound it on to walk forward thro' Eternity." Blake's
Milton, at the close of *Milton*, utters a great declaration in
which the imagery of removing false garments, which goes
through the whole of the poem, achieves an apotheosis:

To cleanse the Face of my Spirit by Self-examination,
To bathe in the Waters of Life; to wash off the Not Human,
I come in Self-annihilation & the grandeur of Inspiration
To cast-off Rational Demonstration by Faith in the Saviour
To cast off the rotten rags of memory by Inspiration
To Cast off Bacon, Locke & Newton from Albions covering
To take off his filthy garments, & clothe him with Imagination
To cast aside from Poetry, all that is not Inspiration . . .

There indeed is the crux: why should Blake's memory of Milton's poetry be one of "the rotten rags of Memory," and can anyone "cast aside from Poetry, all that is not Inspiration"? Memory is not only the principal mode of cognition in poetry; it is also pragmatically the major source of inspiration. Blake has not written *Alexander Pope: A Poem in Two Books* because it is not Pope who has overdetermined him. Milton, and the Bible, have enclosed Blake, rather in the way that Freud now encloses all of us, whether we know it or not. Blake knew his enclosure, yet idealized it in a powerfully productive repression. Whether the product, as in *Milton,* does not fall more toward belief than toward poetry now seems to me much more problematical than it once did. Is *Milton* more the product of the poetic will, of Los the prophet with his hammer "in unpitying ruin driving down the pyramids of pride," or is it the product of Blake's own passional anxiety, of Luvah "reasoning from the loins in the unreal forms of Beulah's night"?

The shadow of Milton, for Blake, had entered the nightmare of history, which includes the representative of that larger nightmare, poetic history. Blake told us that "in Milton; the Father is Destiny, the Son, a Ratio of the five senses, & the Holy-ghost, Vacuum!" I begin to fear that in Blake, the Father is Milton, the Son is Blake, who is a profound reduction of Milton and the Bible, and the Holy Ghost of inspiration is a not wholly persuasive special pleading. Blake, like the poets of sensibility, lingered in that theater of the mind, that *kenoma* or sensible emptiness, which lay between Enlightenment truth and High Romantic meaning. He could not ruin the sacred truths, either to fable and old song, or to a story that might emerge clearly from the abyss of his own strong ego, as it emerged from Wordsworth, even as Blake wrote his own brief epics. Blake is one of the last of an old race of poets; Wordsworth was the very first of the race of poets that we have with us still. Blake is archaic, as perhaps he wanted to be. Wordsworth is more modern than Freud, more postmodern than Samuel Beckett or Thomas Pynchon, because Wordsworth alone found the new way, our way alas, to ruin sacred truths.

ॐ

It is only a decade now since I first read the two-part *Prelude* of 1799, a poem of less than a thousand lines, not published until 1974. Rereading it is an extraordinary experience, partly because of the shock of recontextualization that the poem necessarily provides for any reader who is deeply conversant with *The Prelude* as Wordsworth completed it in 1805, or with the posthumously published work of 1850, which received its curiously misleading title from the poet's widow. For Wordsworth it was always his "poem to Coleridge" and the first part of his projected masterwork, *The Recluse*. There is a happy surprise at finding in one place all the grand "spots of time" passages, yet the aesthetic experience of apprehending the two-part *Prelude* transcends that delight. For nearly a thousand lines you go from strength to strength, with none of those flats and resting places in which the two longer *Prelude*s abound. The first four books of *Paradise Lost,* and the seventh and ninth books also of Milton's epic, are the only comparable instances of such sustained sublimity in the poetry of our language. Perhaps *Night the Ninth, being the Last Judgment* of Blake's *The Four Zoas* is another rival, but *Night the Ninth* goes beyond the sublime by having too direct a design upon us. Going back to the everyday after reading it sometimes gives me that peculiar sensation we all receive when we emerge from a movie matinee into the sunlight of midafternoon on a summer day. Wordsworth gives you a sublime you can live with, and never more gently than in the two-part *Prelude.*

Criticism, Oscar Wilde observed, is the only civilized form of autobiography, and Oscar was always right. I have never felt any particular affinity to Wordsworth, as I did to Blake and

Hart Crane when I was a boy, and as I have to Shelley and to Wallace Stevens ever since I was an undergraduate. I don't think that I have loved Wordsworth's poetry, as I love the poetry of Walt Whitman or of Emily Dickinson, still the strongest poets our country has engendered. But I read Wordsworth pretty much in the personal way I read the Hebrew Bible, looking for consolation, by which I don't mean cheering myself up. As the years pass, I develop an ever greater horror of solitude, of finding myself having to confront sleepless nights and baffled days in which the self ceases to know how to talk to itself. Wordsworth, more than any other single poet, instructs me in how to sustain the heaviness of going on talking to myself. I don't believe that the aging process alone, or the sorrows of the family romance, or the vicissitudes of the drive qualify as the truest sources of our need to relearn perpetually how to talk to ourselves. Freud's only transcendentalism was his exaltation of the reality principle, the disenchanting acceptance of one's own mortality. We all of us have some vestige of Platonism in us. Freud was enchanted by being disenchanted, by the pleasures of ceasing to be deceived. My highest praise of Freud is to say that he is the Wordsworth of our century, a curious observation to make half a century after his death. Proust and Kafka are the central poets of our century, and their legitimate representative abides with us in Samuel Beckett, certainly the crucial living writer in the West. But these last exemplars of the sublime are available to us only as versions of Freud's uncanny, our conceptual limit for the sublime. Freud is our Wordsworth, yet does not cost me Wordsworth, as he has cost me Blake. You do not lose Wordsworth, and I would like to explain why, if I can.

My late teacher Frederick Pottle wrote an essay on Wordsworth and Freud called "The Theology of the Unconscious." I think that is the proper link; neither Wordsworth nor Freud was an unconscious theologian—yet both sought to replace a dying god with a new one, the god of the perpetually growing inner self. That makes them both descendants of my least favorite Biblical proclaimer, the unwholesome Jeremiah, but Wordsworth and Freud were much more benign than the hysterically powerful Jeremiah. Jeremiah had a positive passion for the destruction he lamented, while they had a profound affection for all of us and immense sympathy for our discomfort with culture. Nevertheless, I fear that Wordsworth and Freud were also responsible for writing the Law upon our inward parts, and thus completing the Enlightenment's program of internalizing all values. This seems an unjust indictment in the wake of Wordsworth's insistence upon the progressive and yet further humanization of the human heart by which we live, and of Freud's incessant emphasis upon reality testing. Otherness is the overt teaching of Wordsworth and of Freud, whether the other be the object of the heart's affections or the object of the drives. Yet there is something equivocal in that otherness, whether Freudian or Wordsworthian, because tropologically such otherness itself is a kind of death, a figuration for one's own death.

Our father Freud, in "Mourning and Melancholia," ruminated upon this subtle and dangerous equivocation: "As the primal condition from which instinct-life proceeds we have come to recognize a self-love of the ego which is so immense, in the fear that rises up at the menace of death we see liberated a volume of narcissistic libido which is so vast, that we cannot conceive how this ego can conceive at its own destruction."

Yet what we cannot conceive, the ego certainly does conceive; it creates the inner self. If only the inner self could remain with itself, then all might be well, but Freud ruefully tells us that "ultimately man must begin to love in order not to get ill." Wordsworth tells us the same, with a less overt ruefulness, in the 1805 *Prelude* and later, but not at all in the two-part *Prelude* of 1799, which owes much of its extraordinary power to its sublimely untroubled self-love. What the poem calls nature is authentically an otherness, but an otherness without the distraction of other selves. There is of course Coleridge, to whom the poem is addressed, but he is neither an absence nor a presence; he is Horatio to Wordsworth's Hamlet, and so is a surrogate for the readership. Nature however, as a hard, phenomenal otherness, is scarcely a surrogate for anything, and is strikingly similar to Freud's reality principle, the context that rims the inner self, a context that begins as the universe of sense and ends as the universe of death. If European Enlightenment can be defined as a high rationalism, a confidence in the capacity of our reason to apprehend the world accurately, and through that apprehension to change in it what needs changing, then Wordsworthian nature in one way marks the limit of that Enlightened rationalism. Yet so dialectical is Wordsworth's poetry that in quite another way his vision of nature culminates the Enlightenment program for the reason. The two-part *Prelude* turns continually, like much of the poetry of Wordsworth's great decade, upon the topos of how and to what extent the poet's mind is lord and master, outward sense the servant of the mind's will. Any sublime that founds itself upon the power of the mind over a universe of death must smash itself to fragments on that rock of otherness constituted at last by death our death.

Neurosis, according to Freud, results from attempting to abolish one's personal past; this hardly means that Freud regarded the past as other than an intolerable burden. In Wordsworth the past is not a burden but a force, without which we fall into death-in-life. I take it that this difference is what makes Freud a continuator of the Enlightenment, while Wordsworth is something else, High Romantic as we might now call it. Whether there is a similar difference between Freud and Wordsworth on the otherness of death seems to me more problematic. Since the trope of the father, from the Bible onward, is the only Western trope that participates neither in origins nor in ends, while the trope of the mother pervades both origins and ends, it is very persuasive that Freud explictly associates any death with the way the "whole past stirs within one." Guilt, according to Freud, is always the guilt of having survived the father, presumably because of the repressed wish to have murdered the father. The second "spot of time" passage in *The Prelude* centers upon the death of Wordsworth's father, which occurred in December 1783, five years after the death of the poet's mother. The thirteen-year-old Wordsworth waits upon a ridge, in the company of two of his brothers, for the horses that would bear them home for Christmas:

> 'Twas a day
> Stormy, and rough, and wild, and on the grass
> I sate half sheltered by a naked wall.
> Upon my right hand was a single sheep,
> A whistling hawthorn on my left, and there,
> Those two companions at my side, I watched
> With eyes intensely straining, as the mist
> Gave intermitting prospects of the wood
> And plain beneath. Ere I to school returned
> That dreary time, ere I had been ten days
> A dweller in my father's house, he died,
> And I and my two brothers, orphans then,
> Followed his body to the grave.

Of those two companions by the naked wall, the hawthorn ceased to whistle and became blasted in the revisionary 1850 *Prelude*. The denudation of the scene is crucial, as its chief actors are the weather and the eminence that the thirteen-year-old Wordsworth mounts, which is located at an Oedipal crossroads, "the meeting-point of two highways." The entire passage, like all of the spots of time, has a curiously repressed intensity to it, an excitement of expectation, or anxiety of hope, as the poet soon will call this. That expectation, as if hastening the event, is of the father's death, as Wordsworth could not have known in any conscious sense. Yet this is what follows the image of the funeral procession of the orphans:

> The event,
> With all the sorrow which it brought, appeared
> A chastisement; and when I called to mind
> That day so lately passed, when from the crag
> I looked in such anxiety of hope,
> With trite reflections of morality,
> Yet with the deepest passion, I bowed low
> To God who thus corrected my desires.

God is not very frequently mentioned in *The Prelude*, and He may not be altogether identical with the poem's unnamed third presence that, in moments of crisis, subsumes both nature and Wordsworth's imagination. *The Prelude*, like its nearest ancestor, *Paradise Lost*, is not an Augustinian poem. Saint Augustine after all shared the universe with God, but Milton and Wordsworth were quite alone in the cosmos. Hazlitt, in his "Observations on *The Excursion*," cunningly associated Wordsworth with Milton's revision of Genesis in the invocation of the Holy Spirit: "He may be said to create his own materials; his thoughts are his real subject. His understanding broods over that which is 'without form and void' and makes it pregnant. He sees all things within himself. He hardly ever avails himself of remarkable objects or situations, but, in general, rejects them as interfering with the workings of his own mind, as disturbing the smooth, deep, majestic current of his own feelings."

Because *The Prelude*, more than *The Excursion*, is best interpreted as a strong misreading of *Paradise Lost*, Hazlitt usefully hints at the Protestant stance of imagination shared by Milton, Wordsworth, and himself. It is with a dissenting passion that the boy Wordsworth bows low to a deity that by no means succeeds in correcting a great poet's desires for total self-engendering. What Wordsworth calls God here has much to do with these "trite reflections of morality," while "the deepest passion" is reserved for the mystery of the ever-increasing inner self. That passion is adumbrated in the passage following, which would have been the conclusion of a five-book *Prelude* that Wordsworth contemplated in March 1804:

> And afterwards the wind and sleety rain,
> And all the business of the elements,
> The single sheep, and the one blasted tree,
> And the bleak music of that old stone wall,
> The noise of wood and water, and the mist
> Which on the line of each of those two roads
> Advanced in such indisputable shapes—
> All these were spectacles and sounds to which
> I often would repair, and thence would drink
> As at a fountain. And I do not doubt
> That in this later time, when storm and rain
> Beat on my roof at midnight or by day
> When I am in the woods, unknown to me
> The workings of my spirit thence are brought.

Can we define that fountain? The entire sequence evidently was crucial for Wordsworth, since he thought of stationing it at the poem's conclusion. The spots of time in the two-part *Prelude* are said to "retain a fructifying virtue," while in the 1805 and 1850 *Preludes* "renovating" replaces "fructifying." Helping the mind to bear fruit is a stronger function than renovating it, and perhaps the best title for the two-part poem of 1799 would have been *Spots of Time,* since nothing in the text could fail to sustain that remarkable oxymoron. "Spots" presumably are more or less small, and have precise limits, but such definiteness vanishes when they are "of time." In a famous letter to Walter Savage Landor, Wordsworth expressed a preference for visions in which the edges of things dissolved, with all fixities and densities placed in flux, with limits giving way and expectations being raised. The spots of time are not moments of place, nor do they occur within a place. Beliefs can be localized in a shrine or a similar place, but fructifications demand a temporal continuum. The fountain of spectacles and sounds is not a topos but an event stretching across two times and bearing the past alive into the present. When Wordsworth speaks of the workings of his spirit, he describes not a believing that something is so but a trusting in a covenant, a covenant made between his adverting mind and a subsuming presence not wholly distinct from his own best aspect. What the spots of time testify to is the astonishing extent of the mind's mastery over the universe of death, but such a mind is more than elitist; it is theomorphic. Wordsworth celebrates his own godhood, which is a very vexing assertion, as even I am aware. But what else is the authentic burden of Wordsworth's poetry, unless it be his sense of election to be the prophet of nature, as he calls it, in succession to Milton as prophet of Protestantism? If there is belief in *The Prelude,* or in any other vital poetry of the great decade, it can only be belief in the imaginative strength of one's own divine childhood. Commenting upon his "Intimations of Immortality" ode, Wordsworth was clearer than any exegete can hope to be:

Nothing was more difficult for me in childhood than to admit the notion of death as a state applicable to my own being . . . it was not so much from the source of animal vivacity that *my* difficulty came as from a sense of the indomitableness of the spirit within me. I used to brood over the stories of Enoch and Elijah, and almost persuade myself that, whatever might become of others, I should be translated in something of the same way to heaven. With a feeling congenial to this, I was often unable to think of external things as having external existence, and I communed with all that I saw as something not apart from, but inherent in, my own immaterial nature.

"The indomitableness of the spirit within me" is a Protestant and Miltonic sentiment to Wordsworth, but I think that we must now identify such a stance as Wordsworthian, since he remains our archetype of the strong modern poet. Who since him, in any Western language, has been able to compete with him? For almost two centuries now, Wordsworth has triumphed in the agon of the sublime, despite Hölderlin and Keats, Victor Hugo and Walt Whitman, Browning and Emily Dickinson, and, in our own century, Rilke, Valéry, Yeats, and Wallace Stevens. Increasingly we recognize that something like a continuum runs from Homer to Goethe, and that something else begins with Wordsworth, something that keeps on beginning, despite all the waves of modernism, postmodernism, or what you will. In the longest perspective that we can achieve, the supposedly sober and tame Wordsworth remains the most original and disturbing poet of the nineteenth or the twentieth century. He also seems to me much the most difficult, and not just because he is inexhaustible to meditation. He did what even Blake could not do, and in a sense what even Freud himself could not accomplish, despite the shocking originality of the founder of psychoanalysis. Wordsworth alone made it new, began again not just upon a tabula rasa of poetry, as Hazlitt asserted, but upon a tabula rasa of the representation of human consciousness.

This is not to say that Wordsworth broke with the Locke tradition, with the Enlightenment, but he severely modified the way in which the enlightened mind apprehended the nature and destiny of human consciousness. Reason in its most exalted mood may seem a High Germanic trope when we encounter it in Coleridge, but it again is something else in Wordsworth, who essentially always remained the pre-Coleridgean of "Guilt and Sorrow" rather than a Continental idealist. The Wordsworths of Geoffrey Hartman and Paul de Man alike are dialectical in their negations, but the actual Wordsworth of the great decade still seems to me a Miltonic agonist, contending not with nature, even in its last guise of mortality, but with the sacred Milton himself. Like his agonist and fathering force, the Wordsworth that I read is a monist, beyond heroic vitalism because he does not need so desperate and belated a stance. The two-part *Prelude* of 1799 completes the work of *Paradise Lost* in destroying the distinction between sacred and secular poetry. What it celebrates ultimately is neither nature nor God, and not even a presence transcending Wordsworth's own creative force. Rather, the poem praises Wordsworth's own transport, his own exalted sublimity, the pathos of the Miltonic bard emancipated from any representations that could inhibit the fully imagined self:

> But let this at least
> Be not forgotten, that I still retained
> My first creative sensibility,
> That by the regular action of the world
> My soul was unsubdued. A plastic power
> Abode with me, a forming hand, at times
> Rebellious, acting in a devious mood,
> A local spirit of its own, at war
> With general tendency, but for the most
> Subservient strictly to the external things
> With which it communed. An auxiliar light
> Came from my mind, which on the setting sun
> Bestowed new splendor; the melodious birds,
> The gentle breeze, fountains that ran on
> Murmuring so sweetly in themselves, obeyed
> A like dominion, and the midnight storm
> Grew darker in the presence of my eye.

Hence my obeisance, my devotion hence,
And *hence* my transport.

As if three "hences" were insufficient, Wordsworth italicizes
the final one, so that we may know that the orders of priority
and of authority fuse here in this poet's own "first creative sensibility." "First" takes on its Miltonic meaning of "earliest," as
it does five times in the opening lines of *Paradise Lost*. How
simple it is to substitute Milton's Satan for Wordsworth in
parts of Wordsworth's proclamation of "*hence* my transport":
I still retained my first self-begotten being, / That by the action
of the Heavenly Tyrant, / My soul was subdued. An immortal
power / Abode with me, a forming hand, at times / Rebellious,
acting in a devious mood, / A noble spirit of its own, at war /
With imposed authority. However, Satan departs, and a more
original Wordsworth comes forth, when we observe an "aux-
iliar light" coming from the poet's mind and bestowing new
splendor upon the setting sun, even as it will do at the close of
the "Intimations of Immortality" ode. There is a transumption
here of the figure of the setting sun at the close of *Lycidas*, and
of the blind bard's internalization of the Holy Light in the invocation to Book 3 of *Paradise Lost*. But because we have gone
from the Enlightenment satire of Pope and Swift, through the
counter-Enlightenment of Blake's warning against reasoning
from the loins in the unreal forms of Luvah's night, on to the
truly triumphant egotistical sublime in the preternaturally
strong Wordsworth, I would prefer to close with an American
transumption somewhat more vulnerable than the Wordsworthian transport. Our own American sublime more frankly
exalts poetry over belief, and receives its classical declaration
in an audacious moment of *Song of Myself*, where our own father, Walt Whitman, deliberately turns his back upon Wordsworth and confronts the fearsome sunrise of our evening land.
In the pathos of Walt Whitman, superbly measured and self-

consciously magnificent, we listen to our own reply to tradition's exiles between truth and meaning:

> Dazzling and tremendous, how quick the sunrise would kill
> me,
> If I could not now and always send forth sunlight from
> myself.

VI

FREUD
AND
BEYOND

FREUD speculated that what we first forget, and only subsequently remember, is the most important element in a dream, or perhaps in any other representation of our desires. "Important" here means central for an interpretation. Freud's theory of repression, or unconscious yet purposeful forgetting, is at the center of his vast speculative project. Consequently, we know a great deal about Freudian forgetting, yet remarkably little about what might be termed Freudian remembering. Since Freud's was anything but a psychology of historical changes, we might have expected that his view of people as immutable through the ages would have concerned itself with what most makes for the immutable, which is memory and its discontents. If we have an unchanging nature, then the past should have unchallenged authority for us. But Freud's therapeutic design intends the undoing of our histories. Not only is individual sexuality to be liberated from the family romance, but thought itself is to be freed of its necessarily sexual past—freed at least in a few elite individuals strong enough to bear their own freedom.

Freud refused to study the nostalgias. He hated the past, and he hated the United States, perhaps because he feared that it was the future. But his hatred of America was founded upon ignorance, while he *knew* the past, and so hated it with reason. Jews are urged by their tradition to remember, but very selectively. Freud was peculiarly Jewish, in profound ways that we begin only now to understand. We note and commend Freud's ingenuity in having transformed the initial prime obstacle to psychoanalysis, the transference, into the pragmatic prime instrument of analytical therapy. If there is something ineluctably Jewish about that transformation, then perhaps we can take it as a synecdoche for all the Jewish metamorphoses of exile into achievement. The wandering people has taught itself and others the lesson of wandering meaning, a wandering that has compelled a multitude of changes in the modes of interpretation available to the West. Of these changes, the Freudian speculation has been perhaps the most influential in our century, if only because we now find it difficult to recall that psychoanalysis, after all, is only a speculation, rather than a science, a philosophy, or even a religion. Freud is closer to Proust than to Einstein, closer even to Kafka than to the scientism of Darwin.

What marks the Freudian transference, above all, is ambivalence, which is also the particular mark of Freud's mythological version of the taboo (in his seminal cultural speculation, *Totem and Taboo*). Ambivalence, in Freud's sense, is simultaneous love and hatred directed toward the same object. The transference and the taboo alike are variations upon Freud's central vision of psychic ambivalence, the Oedipus complex. Transforming an obstacle to analysis into a technique of analysis is therefore equivalent to converting the Oedipal intensities from a human burden into a human release. If this element in Freudian praxis truly is indebted to the wisdom of the Diaspora, in very broad cultural terms, then Freud is another of the authors of the Jewish myths of exile, and psychoanalysis becomes another parable of a people always homeless or at least uneasy in space, who must seek a perpetually deferred fulfillment in time.

Whether there is a specifically biblical basis for the Jewish discontent with visual space, and the Jewish creative obsession with hearing in time, is disputable. Most attempts to contrast Hebrew and Greek thought, on the supposed basis of crucial differences between Hebrew and Greek as languages, have been demonstrated to be illusory. Yet the intellectual and spiritual conflict between Jew and Greek is anything but illusory, and indeed still seems irreconcilable. Western conceptualization is Greek, and yet Western religion, however conceptualized, is not. Freud curiously reduced all religion to the longing for the father. Whatever we may think of this reduction, it is not Greek. Nor is the Freudian Eros at all Greek, since Freud interprets every investment of libido as a transaction in the transference of authority, which always resides in figures of the individual's past and only rarely survives in the individual proper. It is not Greek to vacillate between the need to be everything in oneself and the anxiety of being nothing in oneself. That vacillation helps account for what Freud called repression or defense, the flight from forbidden representations of desire. The theory of repression is coherent only in a psychic cosmos where absolutely everything is meaningful, so that a dream or a joke or a symptom or a transference can sustain a level of interpretative intensity akin to the rabbinical procedures for unpacking Torah. "Turn it and turn it, for everything is in it," the sage Ben Bag Bag remarks of Torah in *Pirke Abot*. This aphorism could have served as epigraph to Freud's *The Interpretation of Dreams,* but only because Freud, like the rabbis, had placed everything in the past.

To ask whether there is a specifically Jewish attitude toward time is to ask the even more problematic question: What is it to be Jewish? Does one intend the biblical, or the normatively rabbinical, or something more belated by the question? Three thousand and more years of apparent continuity mask astonishing discontinuities, as many of them ancient as modern. The clearest answer ought to be religious, but the phrase "the Jewish religion" is itself misleading. Generally, the phrase refers to what the Harvard historian of religion, George Foot Moore, first named "normative Judaism": the faith of Akiba and his colleagues in the second century C.E. But they lived perhaps twelve centuries after the Yahwist, greatest and most original of the biblical writers. Between his tales of Abraham, Jacob, Joseph, and Moses, and the rabbis' extraordinary modes of interpretation, there had been many interventions, of which the

most decisive was the influx of Greek culture after Alexander's
world conquests. The oral Torah, created by the rabbis as a defensive hedge around Scripture, is ultimately Platonic in its
function, though not in its ideology. Nothing in the Hebrew
Bible proclaims the holiness of study, or sees the Jewish people
saving themselves, as a people, by Torah learning. Yet this vision of sanctification through instruction has become so Judaic, even so Jewish, that its Platonic origin now constitutes a
shock for almost all Jews, however scholarly. The historical difference between the Yahwist and Akiba *is* Plato, and this influx
of Athens into Jerusalem saved Judaism, and the Jews, from
being scattered into oblivion among the nations, by giving the
Jews a central formulation of their own culture, but in Greek,
the universal language.

Differences between Hebrew and Greek ideas of history
nevertheless abound, though whether those differences can aid
us in separating out distinctive Jewish notions of time and of
memory is problematical, and can be illuminated by Yosef
Hayim Yerushalmi's *Zakhor: Jewish History and Jewish Memory*
(1982). The Hebrew Bible commands the Jews to remember,
because its God is primarily "the God of your fathers, the God
of Abraham, Isaac and Jacob," known only through His historical self-revelations, rather than through the cycles of time,
natural or mythic. Historical time as such does not matter to
Israel; what matters are the times when God intervenes and
Israel responds. Significant time, in this sense, is clearly not a
Greek notion, for a surprising reason that has more to do with
"Israel responds" than with "God intervenes." What is peculiarly Judaic is the faith that God's interventions are always primarily for the purpose of eliciting Israel's response. In this
sense also, the Freudian view of the human predicament remains biblical. Because the intervention is for *our* response, we
can be tempted to believe we are everything; because the inter-
vener is incommensurate with us, we can fear that we are

nothing. The Psalms echo with this most terrible of affective self-contradictions, taking us in a few phrases from lying down among the potsherds to being as the wings of a dove. The Shakespearean view of man is the biblical and now the Freudian view, rather than the Roman stoicism of Seneca. Hamlet's dramatic reveries transcend even the Yahwist and Freud in a dialectical awareness that everything, and yet nothing, is for Hamlet's sake alone, a dialectic that exalts time rather than place, or an interior place only.

A certain curious sense of interiority marks Jewish thought, as a mode that negates all idolatry, all bondage to the bodily eye. The invisible God of the Jews makes only a handful of actual appearances in the Bible, and in only one of those—the Sinai Theophany, where the elders sit, eat, and gaze at Him— does He fail to speak. Appearances account for less in the Bible than in very nearly any other literature, and there must be some connection, however obscured by our estrangement from the Bible, between the devaluation of the eye and the extraordinary text of the Second Commandment:

> You shall not make for yourself a sculptured image, or any likeness of what is in the heavens above, or on the earth below, or in the waters under the earth. For I the Lord your God am an impassioned God, visiting the guilt of the fathers upon the children, upon the third and upon the fourth generations of those who reject Me, but showing kindness to the thousandth generation of those who love Me and keep My commandments.

This zealous or impassioned God molded Adam in His own *zelem* (image) and so presumably He is urging us not to presume to emulate Him, that being the Greek sin of Prometheus or the Romantic sin of Frankenstein. But the prohibition then continues until it becomes remarkably comprehensive, and the divine passion mounts to sublime hyperbole. That the intent of the Second Commandment is to compel us to an extreme interiority is palpable enough, but the very power of this rhetoric encouraged the rebellious Gnostic imagination to an unprecedented originality in the idolatry of fabulation. The preferred biblical way of representing an object is to explain *how it was made*. We are not told how the Ark of the Covenant, the Desert Sanctuary, the Temple, and Solomon's Palace looked, because the stories of how they were built is what constitutes depiction. And though we are told that Joseph, David, and Absalom were outstandingly handsome, again we are given only an impression, with no sense of their actual appearance. Yet the beauty of Absalom is hardly an index to his interiority, except in ways so subtle as to suggest that the great writer who composed 2 Samuel had his own highly original doubt of appearances. The Second Commandment evidently was no inhibition for prose narrative, and perhaps we are wrong to find in it the ancestor of many of the later Jewish anxieties of representation.

Yet some of these do have profound if dialectical connections to the rabbinical tradition which, as Walter Benjamin remarked, chose *not to see*, a legacy he rightly found still alive in Kafka, and which seems to me equally lively in Freud's theories. We are all of us sensitive to the place of the negative in Jewish thought, a sensitivity upon which I wish to expand. Do Freud and Kafka manifest a Jewish version of negation, one highly distinct from the Hegelian mode of negative thinking? Hegelian negation both culminates European rationalism and aggressively sets that rationalism against British empiricism, with its contempt for universals. Herbert Marcuse observed that Hegel's intellectual optimism is based upon a destructive concept of the given, thus denying any empirical insistence upon the ultimate authority of the fact. Freudian *Verneinung* is anything but a Hegelian dialectical negation, alien to Freud both in its optimism and in its transcendence of mere fact. Rather, Freud's negative is dualistic, mingling ambivalently a purely cognitive return of the repressed and a continuation of the repression of all affect, of the flight away from forbidden and yet desired images and memories. We can call Hegelian negation perhaps the most profound of all Gentile idealizations, after Plato, and then say of the Freudian (and Kafkan) mode of negation that always it reenacts the ambiguities of the Second Commandment.

The difference between Hegelian and Freudian *Verneinung* is evaded by French Freudians (Lacan, Deleuze, Laplanche, even Derrida). This evasion invalidates their readings of Freud, since ultimately they destroy his proud dualisms by rendering them into mere "psychical duplicities." Hegelian negation allows the mind to attain the self-consciousness that will free nature, history, and society from the authority of empiricism and positivism. So Marcuse sums up Hegelian truth as "the result of a double process of negation, namely, (1) the negation of the 'per se' existence of the object, and (2) the negation of the individual I with the shifting of the truth to the universal." But Freud, as Richard Wollheim writes, "traced . . . the capacity to assign truth or falsity to an assertion, to some very primitive movement of the mind, in which something like a thought is felt within one," and then it is either projected or introjected. This is certainly not Hegelian, but is very close to what Yerushalmi calls "Jewish memory."

Hegelianizing Freud, whether in the linguistic mode of Lacan or the subtler, more skeptical way of Derrida, ends by undoing his radical dualisms (primary process/secondary process; pleasure principle/reality principle), and by thus driving Freud into a kind of phantasmagoric monism, in which the primal ambivalence of an aggressive narcissism becomes our ruling passion. But if you undo Freud's dualisms, then you confound him with his "renegades"—Jung, Adler, Reich, Rank, all of them what the poet Wallace Stevens called "fundamentalists of the First Idea." True, Freud's First Idea of civil war in the psyche still would be conflictive, but the conflict will tend to take place *within* a narcissistic, mostly unconscious ego, rather than between the ego and the superego, or the ego and the id. That is as large a revision of Freud as Adler was, and if my surmises are accurate, it also removes Freud from the problematical domain of Jewish memory.

We can locate Freud in that domain by first acknowledging the often contradictory and ambiguous relationship between Freud and Judaism, but then subtly associating the biblical and the Freudian ideas of personality and the possibilities of its sublimation. I would add that sublimation, in the Freudian sense, may well be a Jewish ideal, but the true center of Freud's work is the concept of repression, which is profoundly Jewish, and even normatively so. Freudian memory is Jewish memory, and Freudian forgetting is yet more Jewish. Freud's *Verdräng-ung* is now weakly translated by "repression," whose current overtones are misleadingly ideological and even political. But *Verdrängung*, despite its etymology, is not the trope of pushing under or pushing down, but rather the trope of flight, of an estrangement from representations, under the influence of an inner drive.

I come full circle here by returning to the idea of a psychic cosmos, rabbinical and Freudian, in which there is sense in everything, because everything already is in the past, and nothing that matters can be utterly new. Rabbinical memory, as Yerushalmi expounds it, insists that all meanings are present already in the Bible, in its normative commentaries, and in the oral law represented in each generation by the interpreters who stand centrally in the tradition. If everything is there already, then everything in the Bible is absolutely meaningful. Mix together this passion for total intelligibility with a discarding of every mythology, of all idolatry, of the possibility of mere irrationalisms, and you are very close to Freud's own stance regarding individual consciousness (memory). This must be why Freud had the audacity, in the special preface he wrote for the Hebrew version of *Totem and Taboo,* to affirm the inward Jewishness of his science, and to hint even that he might be forming a Judaism for the future. The Second Commandment, in our time, is called primal repression, which now takes place before there is anything to be repressed.

Freud implicitly knew this, and that knowledge underlies his weird late book *The Man Moses,* translated into English as *Moses and Monotheism.* In what Freud himself called "my novel," the Yahwist is so revised as to vanish, and Moses is declared to be an Egyptian, Yahwism thus becoming an Egyptian invention. Freud's motives were at least double: to revitalize the outrageous primal history scene of *Totem and Taboo,* and to remove a major rival for authority. It is worth remarking that Freud eagerly speculated, at just this time, that the Earl of Oxford had written Shakespeare, a curious devaluation of yet another true rival. Though dismissing this "cultural" Freud of totemism and of an Egyptian Moses might be a comfort, the dismissal would have to be uneasy, both because the figurative power of the primal history scene lingers, and because the taboo-and-totem complex is the concealed paradigm for the Freudian therapeutics of the transference.

Nothing could be less Jewish than the primal history scene, which reads like a parody of Blake's *Tiriel,* and which centers upon a primal horde of rival brothers who combine to murder and devour their terrible father, who has taken all the women of the horde for his own. Once slain and digested, the father becomes a venerated ancestor god, Nietzsche's "numinous shadow" of *The Genealogy of Morals.* Ambivalence having been resolved by this grotesquely literal introjection of the father, remorse for the crime against the father begins—a remorse upon which, Freud insists, all culture is founded. Religion, Judaism included, is thus the desire for the dead father, whose name in Judaism alternately might be Yahweh or Moses, or for

some among us now, Sigmund Freud. The dead father, our
father Sigmund Freud remarked, proved mightier than the
living one had been. But Yahweh was the true name of the father: Baal and Moloch were not fathers, and Jesus Christ perpetually is a son and not a brother of Yahweh. Freud's grandest
heresy, from a Judaic perspective, is his transfer of the Hebraic
trope of the fatherhood of Yahweh to the hideous totemic
ancestor god of the primal horde. Yahweh's elective love for
Israel, the center of all Jewish memory, could not be more at
variance with the Freudian account of our erotic attachment to
authority: in Freud authority has no love for us.

Freedom, for Freud, had to be freedom from the past, but
never from time, the Jewish (and Freudian) reality principle.
Pragmatically, Jewish freedom is freedom of interpretation,
though Jewish (and Freudian) memory results in all meaning
being overdetermined. What *is* freedom where everything is
overdetermined, where character is fate, and there are, after all,
no accidents? Freud's scientism, not his Jewishness, led to his
proud embrace of the reductive, but his path out of his own
reductionism proved to be his quite Jewish variety of dualism.
We can state the essence of Judaism to be the desire for justice,
against the world, and the related inwardness of morality such
desire creates. Prophetic dualism is precisely that: Elijah and
Amos stand against the unjust world, and so against all outwardness whatsoever. But this at last is Freud's dualism also:
the psyche is at civil war, but what it wars with, in itself, is the
injustice of outwardness, the defensive disorderings of the
drives, the unnecessary sufferings that rob us of the freedom
that yet can be our time.

This freedom Freud named "negation," and I turn again to
this difficult formulation in his very brief, almost abrupt paper
of that title in 1925. Negation works so as to internalize certain objects of the drive, an internalization that ensues in the
very difficult trope of the bodily ego, which in each of us can

be regarded as the object of our own id. But an internalized object is an even more difficult trope or fiction, justified because Freud's extraordinary ambition is to seek to explain nothing less than the origins of thinking, indeed of thinking as a relatively free process. How can a thought become an object, even if that object has been swallowed up by one's bodily ego? I would say that Freud has found a complex metaphor, in the essence of Jewishness, for the ambivalently mingled introjection and projection that together constitute his concept of negation. Combine a moral obsession with justice and the drive to a progressively greater inwardness, and you get what Freud might have called "the bodily superego," or the personified prophetic conscience.

The Jewish God is a personality and a subjectivity, and only if He is indeed dead is the death of the subject more than a currently fashionable Gallic trope. We can cite Spinoza's wholly Jewish apothegm: "Wisdom is meditation not on death but on life." Spinoza might have quoted the fundamental Jewish admonition of the rabbi Tarphon, in *Pirke Abot*: "You are not required to complete the work, but neither are you free to desist from it." The work cannot be completed in time, yet we must work as if there will be time enough to complete it, "to give time to time," as in a Sephardic proverb. Judaism, never much interested in death, is in consequence hardly a philosophical religion, if philosophy is the study of death. Jacob, who won the name Israel, is in my judgment the most Jewish figure in the Bible, because of his endless struggle for the blessing, which in every sense primarily means *more life*.

And yet, consider what constitutes the highest spiritual achievements of modern Jewry: the speculations of Freud, the stories and parables of Kafka, the recovery of Jewish Gnosis by Gershom Scholem. Freud concludes with the vision of a primal ambivalence; Kafka makes a tendency toward ambiguity into a kind of drive; Scholem opposes to the ritual of rabbinical Judaism, which makes nothing happen, the ritual of the Lurianic Kabbalah, a ritual which is a theurgy: these are hardly celebrations of more life.

The Bible is now the most recalcitrant and difficult of all libraries (we cannot call it a text, though it is text itself). The Bible is anything but universal, however we attempt to listen to it, because it addresses an elite. In the Sinai Theophany, as presented by the Yahwist, we are bewildered by the emotional self-contradictions of God, at once inviting the people up to Him, and yet warning also that if they break through to Him, He may break forth against them. Art does not say to us, even implicitly, "Be like me, but do not dare to be too like me!" Kafka, ambiguously apprehensive of biblical ambiguity, has a very complex sense of how the Bible might or might not give us back our lives, as in this meditation upon the life of Moses: "He is on the rack of Canaan all his life; it is incredible that he should see the land only when on the verge of death. The dying vision of it can only be intended to illustrate how incomplete a moment is human life, incomplete because a life like this could last forever and still be nothing but a moment. Moses fails to enter Canaan not because his life is too short but because it is a human life."

We are of the age of Freud and Kafka, who may not have wanted to become Jewish culture, but who nevertheless have redefined that culture for us. Freud and Kafka remind us, less historically than Yerushalmi does in *Zakhor,* that all contemporary Jewish intellectuals are compelled to recognize that they are products of a rupture with their tradition, however much they long for continuity. What could that continuity hope to be, except a form of rupture, another breaking of the vessels? We no longer know just what makes a book Jewish, or a person Jewish, because we have no authority to instruct us as to what is or is not Jewish thought. Jewish thought strongly sets itself against idolatry, but this Jewish stance raises again the problem of whether an aesthetic humanism is not one of the most available modes of idolatry—an accusation that has been made against my own work by some claiming to speak with authority in Jewish matters. I am content to entrust my own defense to the more-than-ironic ambiguity of Kafka: "Abraham falls victim to the following illusion: he cannot stand the uniformity of this world. Now the world is known, however, to be uncommonly various, which can be verified at any time by taking a handful of world and looking at it closely. Thus this complaint at the uniformity of the world is really a complaint at not having been mixed profoundly enough with the diversity of the world."

Since the Jews, the Christians, and the Muslims are all children of Abraham, all Western religion is slyly traced to an illusion of uniformity. What seemed monotonous repetition to Father Abraham may have been a product of his own myopia, the failure to scrutinize a handful of world closely enough. But such scrutiny always robs us of the motive for metaphor, the desire to be different, the desire to be elsewhere, which is Nietzsche's nomadic genealogy of the aesthetic impulse. Kafka's is too formidable an ambiguity to turn fairly against any other modern Jewish thinker, with the single exception of Freud (unless Proust is to be claimed as another such thinker). The Kafkan ambiguity is very uneasy when turned against Freud. To call Freud the Rashi of contemporary Jewish anxieties, as Kafka did, is to compliment even Rashi too highly.

Freud inevitably pervades all of modern Jewish thought, indeed all modern thought. Brooding on the Moses of Michelangelo, Freud found in the piece "a concrete expression of the highest mental achievement that is possible in a man, that of struggling successfully against an inward passion for the sake of a cause to which he has devoted himself." The inward passion here is the justified prophetic wrath that would break the tablets of the Law, and so Freud reads in this Moses his own lineaments. What can struggle successfully against so inward a passion is a freedom even more inward, the freedom of the Law, of Torah, "of the highest mental achievement." We write now not in the freedom of the Law, which is reserved for an Abraham or a Freud, but in a still traditional Jewish freedom. This once was called the freedom to move from the broken tablets to the free tablets.

What *is* most Jewish about Freud's work? I am not much impressed by the answers to this question that follow the pattern from Oedipus to Moses, and thus center themselves upon Freud's own Oedipal relation to his father Jakob. Such answers tell me only that Freud had a Jewish father, and doubtless books and essays yet will be written hypothesizing Freud's relation to his indubitably Jewish mother. Nor am I persuaded by any attempts to relate Freud to esoteric Jewish traditions. As a speculator, Freud may be said to have founded a kind of gnosis, but there are no Gnostic elements in the Freudian dualism. Nor am I convinced by any of the attempts to connect Freud's dream book to supposed Talmudic antecedents. And yet the center of Freud's work, his concept of repression, as I've remarked, does seem to me profoundly Jewish, and in its patterns even normatively Jewish. Freudian memory and Freudian forgetting are a very Jewish memory and a very Jewish forgetting. It is their reliance upon a version of Jewish memory, a parody version if you will, that makes Freud's writings profoundly and yet all too originally Jewish.

To be originally Jewish and yet to be original is a splendid paradox, as Freudian as it is Kafkan. Perhaps one has to be Freud or Kafka to embody such a paradox, and perhaps all that I am saying reduces to this and this alone: the mystery or problem of originality, peculiarly difficult in the context of the oldest, more or less continuous tradition in the West.

Freud obsessively collected classical artifacts, and yet toward the Greeks and the Romans, as toward the Christians, Freud spiritually was not even ambivalent. As a speculator, Freud had come to replace all Gentile anteriority whatsoever. But toward Jewish anteriority Freud indeed was ambivalent. Yahweh, in Freudian terms, had to represent the universal longing for the father, but Freud's own internalization of Yahweh issued at last in the most Jewish of his psychic agencies, the superego. To argue against an old vulgarism with a new one, the ego may be the Gentile but the id is not the Yid. As the "above-I," the superego has no transcendental element or function. It is not a reality instructor for the hapless ego, but something much darker. In his late book that we know as *Civilization and Its Discontents,* Freud writes a kind of tragicomedy or even apocalyptic farce, in which the superego compels the ego to abandon its aggressivities, but then goes on punishing the ego for supposedly manifesting precisely those aggressivities.

This sadomasochistic scenario is a parody of the role of the prophets and of their precursor, Moses, in regard to the ancient Israelites. But it is also an allegory, not so parodistic, of Freud's vision of his own function, as exemplary Jew, in regard to Gentile culture, of which he belatedly regarded Jung as too true a representative. We are again almost in the grotesque plot of *Moses and Monotheism.* There, in a kind of absurdist revision of Freud's primal history scene from *Totem and Taboo,* the Jews murder Moses the Egyptian, who thenceforth becomes, in effect, their superego. Freud's account of Saint Paul then internalizes this superego further through the concept of original sin, thus setting up Christianity as the religion of the son against Judaism as the religion of the father. In one of the most striking of Freudian leaps, Christian anti-Semitism, with its accusation of deicide, is exposed as a polytheistic rebellion against the triumph of the Mosaic and so Jewish superego: "under the thin veneer of Christianity they have remained what their ancestors were, barbarically polytheistic. They have not yet overcome their grudge against the new religion which was forced on them, and they have projected it onto the source from which Christianity came to them. The fact that the Gospels tell a story which is enacted among Jews, and in truth treats only of Jews, has facilitated such a projection. The hatred for Judaism is at bottom hatred for Christianity . . . "

Whether this is convincing is a matter quite apart from its ethos, which is positively Judaistic. After all, why should monotheism be considered an advance upon polytheism, in strictly Freudian terms? Is one really more rational, let alone scientistic, than the other? Manifestly, Freud thought so. But is "thought" really the right word? Freud's obsession with Moses was complex, and the element of identification in it is therefore very difficult to interpret. Still, as I have written elsewhere, Freud's hidden model for the analytical transference was his own mythopoeic account of the taboo, and his even more hidden model for the analyst was his rather frightening vision of the totem-father.

Freud's curious emphasis in *Totem and Taboo* has the effect of somehow Judaising animism, almost as though the Yahwist were composing *The Origin of Species*. What turns out to be most Jewish in Freud is the Yahweh in whom Freud overtly did not care to believe.

In Freud, as I have observed, all love reduces to love of authority or of the father, whom Freud identified ultimately with the Jewish God. Kafka and Scholem knew better than to make such an identification. I argue in my meditation on Kafka that Yahweh is not an authority, which after all is a Roman conception and not a Jewish one. An authority founds and augments, as Freud founded and augmented, but Yahweh is a creator, a revealer, and a redeemer, whose attributes yield us the blessings of more life, rather than those that ensue from the foundation and augmentation of institutions. Freud may be said to have assimilated Mommsen on Roman law to Helmholz on physical law, and then to have compounded both with his own vision of the Egyptian Moses as founder and augmenter of Judaism. This vision is the mythological form of Freud's most curious invention, the analytic transference, the false Eros induced by Freud and his followers for therapeutic purposes, or as a fresh wound inflicted supposedly to heal a wound.

Foucault once observed that Marxism swims in nineteenth-century thought as a fish swims in the sea. One could not make the same remark about what I suggest we begin to call the Freudian speculation. Though Freud emerged from the age of Darwin, he is a curiously timeless figure, as old as Jewish memory. His Jewishness is far more central to him than he cared to believe and, together with Kafka's, may be retrospectively definitive of what Jewish culture can still be as the end of this century approaches. Gershom Scholem, who loved Kafka's writings and rather resented Freud's, said of Kafka's that they had for certain readers (like Scholem) "something of the strong light of the canonical, of that perfection which destroys." For certain other readers Freud's writings share that quality with Kafka's. Though barely touched by normative Judaism, Freud and Kafka were Jewish writers, just as Scholem was. Someday, perhaps, all three together will be seen as having redefined Jewish culture among them.

Freud, in his overt polemic against religion, insisted, as I've noted, upon reducing all religion to the longing for the father. This reduction makes sense only in a Hebraic universe of discourse, where authority always resides in figures of the individual's past and only rarely survives in the individual proper. The Greek spirit encouraged an individual agon for contemporary authority, an agon made possible by the example of the Homeric heroes. But if the hero is Abraham or Jacob rather than Achilles or Odysseus, he provides a much more anxious example. Plato was ironically Homeric in entering upon a struggle with Homer for the mind of Athens, but the Rabbi Akiba would never have seen himself as struggling with Moses for the mind of Jerusalem. Zeus was not incommensurate with the godlike Achilles. Abraham, arguing with Yahweh on the road to Sodom, haggled with God over the number of righteous men required to prevent the destruction of the city but knew he was nothing in himself when face to face with Yahweh. Yet in his humane desperation, Father Abraham pragmatically needed to act momentarily as if he were everything in himself.

Already, Abraham was Freudian man, which is only to say that Freud's conception of the human is surprisingly biblical. Few questions of spiritual or intellectual history are as vexed as the Jewishness of Freud. It mystified Freud, more than he knew, and we go on weakly misreading it. We ought to judge it in relation to Freud's profound and unstated assumptions: convictions about time, memory, hierarchy, rationality, ethics, morality, continuity, above all ambivalence toward the self and toward others. Jewish dualism is neither the split between body and soul nor the abyss between subject and object. Rather it is the ceaseless agon within the self not only against all outward injustice but also against what I have called the injustice of outwardness, or, more simply, the way things are. The *Nevi'im* or prophets inherit the Torah's skeptical inwardness, a spirit that drove Abraham upon his original journey, and that fostered the Second Commandment's rejection of all outward appearances. What appears to be most original in Elijah and in all his descendants down through Malachi is the exaltation of skeptical inwardness as the true mode of preparing to receive the God-word. When a prophet says "The God-word was to me," everything turns upon the meaning of that "me." It is not meaning but will that gets started when Yahweh speaks. Meaning is there already in the prophetic "me," which as an ego is far closer to what we might call the psychoanalytic ego than to the Romantic ego of nineteenth- and twentieth-century Western philosophy and literature. The Romantic ego is the product of, and the protest against, a double split in consciousness, between the adverting mind and its object in nature, and between the mind and the body it inhabits. But the psychoanalytic ego is indeed what Freud calls "the bodily ego"; as he says, "The Ego is first and foremost a bodily Ego." What this rather profoundly means is that the ego frames itself on the paradigm of the human body, so that all the processes of the ego frame themselves also upon the paradigm of the body's processes. Human sexual activity and human cognition alike thus model themselves upon the processes of eating, or excreting, or the stimulation of the genitalia. The consequence is that sexual intercourse and thinking can be assimilated to one another, and to the specific locations of mouth, anus, genitals.

To visualize the ego as a body is to admit the image that pictures the ego physically ingesting the object of the drive, the image of introjection or swallowing up the object. In *The Ego and the Id* (1923), Freud told us that the bodily ego "is not merely a surface entity, but is itself the projection of a surface." Freud's remark, as he apparently recognized, is quite difficult, and he evidently authorized an explanatory footnote in the English translation of 1927, which however does not appear in any of the German editions. The footnote reminds us that the ego ultimately derives from bodily sensations, particularly sensations springing from the surface of the body. Is the bodily ego then a mental projection of the body's surface? Where would the frontier between body and psyche be in such a projection? Like the Freudian concept of the drive, the notion of the bodily ego seems to lie precisely on the frontier between the mental and the physical. Presumably, we can know neither the body nor the bodily ego; we can know only the drives and the defenses. Freud implies that the drives and the bodily ego alike are constructed ambivalently; that is to say, from their origins they are dualistic. In both, the borders between the psychical and the somatic are forever in dispute.

I want to go back a long way in finding a similar vision of ambivalence. Freud, of course, was willing to go back to Empedocles and Heraclitus. I think Freud was closer even to Jeremiah, doubtless unknowingly, and I repeat that ancient Jewish dualism does not oppose body to spirit, or nature to mind, but rather sets outwardness against inwardness. Jeremiah, rather than Freud, is the initial discoverer of the bodily ego, of an untraceable border between selfhood and the somatic. For the romantic ego, whether in Hegel or Emerson, the body is part of the Not-Me. But for Freud, as for Jeremiah, the body is uneasily part of the Me, and not part of the external world. The drive, which excites from within and so menaces the ego, is a somatic demand upon the psyche, and is very different from an external excitation of any kind. When Freud speaks of the psyche's surface, he means perception and consciousness, and he founds this meaning upon what we commonly try to mean when we speak of the surface of the body.

Freud could speak of the bodily ego or the drives or even the defense of introjection as *frontier* concepts only because his image of the ego was that of the body, of a living organism. A body can be attacked and penetrated from without; it has a demarcation that needs defense, and can be defended. The bodily ego could as well have been called the egoistic body, because Freud's crucial metaphor is that of inwardness itself. "Inwardness" is the true name of the bodily ego. The defensive disorderings of the drive, or the vicissitudes of instinct, are figures of outwardness, or of what the prophet Jeremiah might have called the "injustice of outwardness."

In Chapter 20 of Jeremiah, the prophet laments to God that God has enticed him, and has overcome him, so as to make Jeremiah a mockery. But if Jeremiah seeks to speak no more in God's name:

Then there is in my heart as it were a burning fire
Shut up in my bones,
And I weary myself to hold it in,
But cannot.

The burning fire or inwardness drives outward, in a movement that culminates in the magnificence of Chapter 31, where
God speaks of the days coming when he will make a new covenant with the house of Israel, in which all outwardness will be
abolished: "I will put My law in their inward parts, and in
their heart will I write it." Call this the ancient Jewish negation
of the outward, since it is a new perspective upon the genesis
of the ego. Indeed, it is a privileged perspective that has no
relation to the external world. The drive out from inwardness,
from the Freudian id, takes the ego as its object; it does not
generate the ego. Doubtless, a strict psychoanalytic reading
of Jeremiah would say that he is manic, and stretches his own
ego until it introjects God, or the ego ideal, whereas earlier
Jeremiah had been depressive and melancholic, projecting his
own ego out of self-hatred and self-abandonment. But such
clinical judgment, whether accurate or not, is less vital than the
striking similarity between Jeremiah's negative dualism and
Freud's. Both erase the frontier between psyche and body and
in its place install a narcissistic ambivalence. The difficult concept of the bodily ego, in which an imaginary object is introjected as though it were real, is uncannily similar to the
prophetic concept of the placing of the Law in our inward
parts. Surely we have underestimated the conceptual difficulties of the bodily ego. How after all can a thought become
an object, when the bodily ego has introjected it? How can the
Law be inscribed upon our inward parts?

I observed earlier elsewhere that the superego, rather than
the ego, let alone the id, is in some sense the most Jewish of
the psychic agencies. I have ventured also that repression is in
a complex way a peculiarly Jewish notion, related as it is to the

programmatic sorrows of Jewish memory. I conclude this meditation, though, by venturing that Freud's most profound Jewishness, voluntary and involuntary, was his consuming passion for interpretation, a passion that led him into the wilderness of his frontier concepts. The psychical representative of the drive not in the individual consciousness but in human history, allegorically or ironically considered, is the image of a wandering exile, propelled onward in time by all the vicissitudes of injustice and outwardness, all the bodily oppressiveness that is inflicted upon the representatives of interpretation itself, as they make their way along the frontiers between mind and body, known and unknown, past and future, illuminated only flickeringly by the strong light of the canonical, as our ancestors learned to call it, the light of the perfection that destroys.

In her obituary for her lover, Franz Kafka, Milena Jesenská sketched a modern Gnostic, a writer whose vision was of the *kenoma*, the cosmic emptiness into which we have been thrown: "he was a hermit, a man of insight who was frightened by life . . . He saw the world as being full of invisible demons which assail and destroy defenseless man . . . All his works describe the terror of mysterious misconceptions and guiltless guilt in human beings."

Milena—brilliant, fearless, and loving—may have subtly distorted Kafka's beautifully evasive slidings between normative Jewish and Jewish Gnostic stances. Max Brod, responding to Kafka's now-famous remark—"We are nihilistic thoughts that came into God's head"—explained to his friend the Gnostic notion that the Demiurge had made this world both sinful and evil. "No," Kafka replied, "I believe we are not such a radical relapse of God's, only one of His bad moods. He had a bad day." Playing straight man, the faithful Brod asked if this meant there was hope outside our cosmos. Kafka smiled, and charmingly said: "Plenty of hope—for God—no end of hope—only not for us."

Kafka, despite Gershom Scholem's authoritative attempts to claim him for Jewish Gnosticism, is both more and less than a Gnostic, as we might expect. Yahweh can be saved, and the divine degradation that is fundamental to Gnosticism is not an element in Kafka's world. But we were fashioned out of clay during one of Yahweh's bad moods; perhaps there was divine dyspepsia, or sultry weather in the garden that Yahweh had planted in the East. Yahweh is hope, and we are hopeless. We are the jackdaws or crows, the *kafkas* (since that is what the name means, in Czech) whose impossibility is what the heavens signify. "The crows maintain that a single crow could destroy the heavens. Doubtless that is so, but it proves nothing against the heavens, for the heavens signify simply: the impossibility of crows."

In Gnosticism, there is an alien, wholly transcendent God, and the adept, after considerable difficulties, can find the way back to presence and fullness. Gnosticism therefore is a religion of salvation, though the most negative of all such saving visions. Kafkan spirituality offers no hope of salvation, and so is not Gnostic. But Milena Jesenská certainly was right to emphasize the Kafkan terror that is akin to Gnosticism's dread of the *kenoma*, which is the world governed by the Archons. Kafka takes the impossible step beyond Gnosticism, by denying that there is hope for us anywhere at all.

In the aphorisms that Brod rather misleadingly entitled "Reflections on Sin, Pain, Hope and the True Way," Kafka wrote: "What is laid upon us is to accomplish the negative; the positive is already given." How much Kabbalah Kafka knew is not clear. Since he wrote a new Kabbalah, the question of Jewish Gnostic sources can be set aside. Indeed, by what seems a charming oddity (but I would call it yet another proof of

Blake's contention that forms of worship are chosen from poetic tales), our understanding of Kabbalah is Kafkan anyway,
since Kafka profoundly influenced Gershom Scholem, and no
one will be able to get beyond Scholem's creative or strong
misreading of Kabbalah for decades to come. I repeat this point
to emphasize its shock value: we read Kabbalah, via Scholem,
from a Kafkan perspective, even as we read human personality
and its mimetic possibilities by way of Shakespeare's perspec-
tives, since essentially Freud mediates Shakespeare for us, yet
relies upon him nevertheless. A Kafkan facticity or contingency now governs our awareness of whatever in Jewish cultural tradition is other than normative.

In his diaries for 1922, Kafka meditated, on January 16,
upon "something very like a breakdown," in which it was "impossible to sleep, impossible to stay awake, impossible to endure life, or, more exactly, the course of life." The vessels were
breaking for him as his daemonic, writerly inner world and
the outer life "split apart, and they do split apart, or at least
clash in a fearful manner." Late in the evening, K. arrives at the
village, which is deep in snow. The Castle is in front of him,
but even the hill upon which it stands is veiled in mist and
darkness, and there is not a single light visible to show that the
Castle is there. K. stands a long time on a wooden bridge that
leads from the main road to the village, while gazing not at the
village but "into the illusory emptiness above him," where the
Castle should be. He does not know what he will always refuse
to learn, which is that the emptiness is illusory in every possible sense, since he does gaze at the *kenoma*, which resulted
initially from the breaking of the vessels, the splitting apart of
every world, inner and outer.

Writing the vision of K., Kafka counts the cost of his confirmation, in a passage prophetic of Scholem, but with a difference that Scholem sought to negate by combining Zionism

and Kabbalah for himself. Kafka knew better, perhaps only for himself, but perhaps for others as well:

> This pursuit, originating in the midst of men, carries one in a direction away from them. The solitude that for the most part has been forced on me, in part voluntarily sought by me—but what was this if not compulsion too?—is now losing all its ambiguity and approaches its denouement. Where is it leading? The strongest likelihood is that it may lead to madness; there is nothing more to say, the pursuit goes right through me and rends me asunder. Or I can—can I?—manage to keep my feet somewhat and be carried along in the wild pursuit. Where, then, shall I be brought? "Pursuit," indeed, is only a metaphor. I can also say, "assault on the last earthly frontier," an assault, moreover, launched from below, from mankind, and since this too is a metaphor, I can replace it by the metaphor of an assault from above, aimed at me from above.
>
> All such writing is an assault on the frontiers; if Zionism had not intervened, it might easily have developed into a new secret doctrine, a Kabbalah. There are intimations of this. Though of course it would require genius of an unimaginable kind to strike root again in the old centuries, or create the old centuries anew and not spend itself withal, but only begin to flower forth.

Consider Kafka's three metaphors, which he so knowingly substitutes for one another. The pursuit is of ideas, in that mode of introspection which is Kafka's writing. Yet this metaphor of pursuit is also a piercing "right through me" and a breaking apart of the self. For pursuit, Kafka then substitutes mankind's assault, from below, on the last earthly frontier. What is that frontier? It must lie between us and the heavens. Kafka, the crow or jackdaw, by writing, transgresses the frontier and implicitly maintains that he could destroy the heavens. By another substitution, the metaphor changes to "an assault from above, aimed at me from above," the aim simply being the signifying function of the heavens, which is to mean the impossibility of Kafkas or crows. The heavens assault Kafka *through his writing;* "all such writing is an assault on the frontiers," and these must now be Kafka's own frontiers. One thinks of Freud's most complex frontier concept, more complex even than the drive: the bodily ego. The heavens assault Kafka's bodily ego, *but only through his own writing.* Certainly such an assault is not un-Jewish, and has as much to do with normative as with esoteric Jewish tradition.

Yet, according to Kafka, his own writing, were it not for the intervention of Zionism, might easily have developed into a new Kabbalah. How are we to understand that curious statement about Zionism as the blocking agent that prevents Franz Kafka from becoming another Isaac Luria? Kafka darkly and immodestly writes: "There are intimations of this." Our teacher Gershom Scholem governs our interpretation here, of necessity. Those intimations belong to Kafka alone, or perhaps to a select few in his immediate circle. They cannot be conveyed to Jewry, even to its elite, because Zionism has taken the place of messianic Kabbalah, including presumably the heretical Kabbalah of Nathan of Gaza, prophet of Sabbatai Zevi and of all his followers down to the blasphemous Jacob Frank. Kafka's influence upon Scholem is decisive here, for Kafka already has arrived at Scholem's central thesis of the link between the Kabbalah of Isaac Luria, the messianism of the Sabbatarians and Frankists, and the political Zionism that gave rebirth to Israel.

Kafka goes on, most remarkably, to disown the idea that he possesses "genius of an unimaginable kind," one that either would strike root again in archaic Judaism, presumably of the esoteric sort, or more astonishingly "create the old centuries anew," which Scholem insisted Kafka had done. But can we speak, as Scholem tried to speak, of the Kabbalah of Franz Kafka? Is there a new secret doctrine in the superb stories and the extraordinary parables and paradoxes, or did not Kafka spend his genius in the act of new creation of the old Jewish centuries? Kafka certainly would have judged himself harshly as one spent withal, rather than as a writer who "only then began to flower forth."

Kafka died only two and a half years after this meditative moment, died alas just before his forty-first birthday. Yet as the propounder of a new Kabbalah, he had gone very probably as far as he (or anyone else) could go. No Kabbalah, be it that of Moses de Leon, Isaac Luria, Moses Cordovero, Nathan of Gaza, or Gershom Scholem, is exactly easy to interpret, but Kafka's secret doctrine, if it exists at all, is designedly uninterpretable. My working principle in reading Kafka is to observe that he did everything possible to evade interpretation, which only means that what most needs and demands interpretation in Kafka's writing is its perversely deliberate evasion of interpretation. Erich Heller's formula for getting at this evasion is: "Ambiguity has never been considered an elemental force; it is precisely this in the stories of Franz Kafka." Perhaps, but evasiveness is not the same literary quality as ambiguity.

Evasiveness is purposive; it writes between the lines, to borrow a fine trope from Leo Strauss. What does it mean when a quester for a new negative, or perhaps rather a revisionist of an old negative, resorts to the evasion of every possible interpretation as his central topic or theme? Kafka does not doubt guilt, but wishes to make it "possible for men to enjoy sin without guilt, almost without guilt," by reading Kafka. To enjoy sin almost without guilt is to evade interpretation, in exactly the dominant Jewish sense of interpretation. Jewish tradition, whether normative or esoteric, never teaches you to ask Nietzsche's question: "Who is the interpreter, and what power does he seek to gain over the text?" Instead, Jewish tradition asks: Is the interpreter in the line of those who seek to build a hedge about the Torah in every age? Kafka's power of evasiveness is not a power over his own text, and it does build a hedge about the Torah in our age. Yet no one before Kafka built up that hedge wholly out of evasiveness, not Maimonides or Judah Halevi or even Spinoza. Subtlest and most evasive of all writers, Kafka remains the severest and most harassing of the belated sages of what will yet become the Jewish cultural tradition of the future.

The jackdaw or crow or *kafka* is also the weird figure of the great hunter Gracchus (whose Latin name also means "crow"), who is not alive but dead, yet who floats like one living on his death-bark forever. When the fussy Burgomaster of Riva in *The Hunter Gracchus* knits his brow and asks, "And you have no part in the other world (*das Jenseits*)?" the Hunter replies, with grand defensive irony: "I am forever on the great stair that leads up to it. On that infinitely wide and spacious stair I clamber about, sometimes up, sometimes down, sometimes on the right, sometimes on the left, always in motion. The Hunter has been turned into a butterfly. Do not laugh."

Like the Burgomaster, we do not laugh. Being a single crow, Gracchus would be enough to destroy the heavens, but he will never get there. Instead, the heavens signify his impossibility, the absence of crows or hunters, and so he has been turned into another butterfly, which is all we can be, from the perspective of the heavens. And we bear no blame for that:

> "I had been glad to live and I was glad to die. Before I stepped aboard, I joyfully flung away my wretched load of ammunition, my knapsack, my hunting rifle that I had always been proud to carry, and I slipped into my winding sheet like a girl into her marriage dress. I lay and waited. Then came the mishap."
>
> "A terrible fate," said the Burgomaster, raising his hand defensively. "And you bear no blame for it?"
>
> "None," said the Hunter. "I was a hunter; was there any sin

in that? I followed my calling as a hunter in the Black Forest, where there were still wolves in those days. I lay in ambush, shot, hit my mark, flayed the skin from my victims: was there any sin in that? My labors were blessed. 'The Great Hunter of Black Forest' was the name I was given. Was there any sin in that?"

"I am not called upon to decide that," said the Burgomaster, "but to me also there seems to be no sin in such things. But then, whose is the guilt?"

"The boatman's," said the Hunter. "Nobody will read what I say here, no one will come to help me; even if all the people were commanded to help me, every door and window would remain shut, everybody would take to bed and draw the bed-clothes over his head, the whole earth would become an inn for the night. And there is sense in that, for nobody knows of me, and if anyone knew he would not know where I could be found, and if he knew where I could be found, he would not know how to deal with me, he would not know how to help me. The thought of helping me is an illness that has to be cured by taking to one's bed."

How admirable Gracchus is, even when compared to the Homeric heroes! They know, or think they know, that to be alive, however miserable, is preferable to being the foremost among the dead. But Gracchus wishes only to be himself, happy to be a hunter when alive, joyful to be a corpse when dead: "I slipped into my winding sheet like a girl into her marriage dress." So long as everything happens in good order, Gracchus is more than content. The guilt must be the boatman's, and may not exceed mere incompetence. Being dead and yet still articulate, Gracchus is beyond help: "The thought of helping me is an illness that has to be cured by taking to one's bed."

When he gives the striking trope of the whole earth closing down like an inn for the night with the bedclothes drawn over everybody's head, Gracchus renders the judgment "And there is sense in that." There is sense in that only because in Kafka's world as in Freud's, or in Scholem's, or in any world deeply informed by Jewish memory, there is necessarily sense in everything, total sense, even though Kafka refuses to aid you in getting at it or close to it.

But what kind of a world is that, where there is sense in everything, where everything seems to demand interpretation? There can be sense in everything, as J. H. van den Berg once wrote against Freud's theory of repression, only if everything is already in the past and there never again can be anything wholly new. That is certainly the world of the great normative rabbis of the second century C.E., and consequently it has been the world of most Jews ever since. Torah has been given, Talmud has risen to complement and interpret it, other interpretations in the chain of tradition are freshly forged in each generation, but the limits of Creation and of Revelation are fixed in Jewish memory. There is sense in everything because all sense is present already in the Hebrew Bible, which by definition must be totally intelligible, even if its fullest intelligibility will not shine forth until the Messiah comes.

Gracchus, hunter and jackdaw, is Kafka, pursuer of ideas and jackdaw, and the endless, hopeless voyage of Gracchus is Kafka's passage, partly through a language not his own, and largely through a life not much his own. Kafka was studying Hebrew intensively while he wrote "The Hunter Gracchus," early in 1917, and I think we may call the voyages of the dead but never buried Gracchus a trope for Kafka's belated study of his ancestral language. He was still studying Hebrew in the spring of 1923, with his tuberculosis well advanced, and down to nearly the end he longed for Zion, dreaming of receiving his health and firmly grounding his identity by journeying to Palestine. Like Gracchus, he experienced life-in-death, though unlike Gracchus he achieved the release of total death.

"The Hunter Gracchus" as a story or extended parable is not

the narrative of a Wandering Jew or Flying Dutchman, because Kafka's trope for his writing activity is not so much a
wandering or even a wavering, but rather a repetition, labyrin-
thine and burrow-building. His writing repeats not itself but
a Jewish esoteric interpretation of Torah that Kafka himself
scarcely knows, or even needs to know. What this interpretation tells Kafka is that there is no written Torah but only an
oral one. However, Kafka has no one to tell him what this oral
Torah is. He substitutes his own writing therefore for the oral
Torah not made available to him. He is precisely in the stance
of the Hunter Gracchus, who concludes by saying: "I am here,
more than that I do not know, further than that I cannot go.
My ship has no rudder, and it is driven by the wind that blows
in the undermost regions of death."

"What is the Talmud if not a message from the distance?"
Kafka wrote to Robert Klopstock on December 19, 1923.
What was all of Jewish tradition, to Kafka, except a message
from an endless distance? That is surely part of the burden of
the famous parable "An Imperial Message," which concludes
with you, the reader, sitting at your window when evening
falls and dreaming to yourself the parable, which is that God,
in his act of dying, has sent you an individual message. Heinz
Politzer read this as a Nietzschean parable, and so fell into
the trap set by the Kafkan evasiveness: "Describing the fate
of the parable in a time depleted of metaphysical truths, the
imperial message has turned into the subjective fantasy of a
dreamer who sits at a window with a view on a darkening
world. The only real information imported by this story is the
news of the Emperor's death. This news Kafka took over from
Nietzsche . . ."

No, for even though you dream the parable, the parable
conveys truth. The Talmud does exist; it really is an imperial

message from the distance. The distance is too great; it cannot reach you; there is hope, but not for you. Nor is it so clear that God is dead. He is always dying, yet always whispers a message into the angel's ear. It is said to you that "Nobody could fight his way through here even with a message from a dead man," but the Emperor actually does not die in the text of the parable.

Distance is part of Kafka's crucial notion of the negative, which is not a Hegelian nor a Heideggerian negative, but is very close to Freud's negation and also to the negative imaging carried out by Scholem's Kabbalists. But I want to postpone Kafka's Jewish version of the negative until later. "The Hunter Gracchus" is an extraordinary text, but it is not wholly characteristic of Kafka at his strongest, at his uncanniest or most sublime.

When he is most himself, Kafka gives us a continuous inventiveness and originality that rival Dante and truly challenge Proust and Joyce as the dominant Western authors of our century—setting Freud aside, since Freud ostensibly is science and not narrative or mythmaking, though if you believe that, then you can be persuaded of anything. Kafka's beast fables are rightly celebrated, but his most remarkable fabulistic being is neither animal nor human, but is little Odradek, in the curious sketch, less than a page and a half long, "The Cares of a Family Man," whose title might have been translated: "The Sorrows of a Paterfamilias." The family man narrates these five paragraphs, each a dialectical lyric in itself, beginning with one that worries the meaning of the name:

> Some say the word Odradek is of Slavonic origin, and try to account for it on that basis. Others again believe it to be of German origin, only influenced by Slavonic. The uncertainty of both interpretations allows one to assume with justice that neither is accurate, especially as neither of them provides an intelligent meaning of the word.

This evasiveness was overcome by the scholar Wilhelm Emrich, who traced the name Odradek to the Czech word *udraditi,* meaning to dissuade someone from doing anything. Like Edward Gorey's Doubtful Guest, Odradek is uninvited yet will not leave, since implicitly he dissuades you from doing anything about his presence; or, rather, something about his very uncanniness advises you to let him alone:

> No one, of course, would occupy himself with such studies if there were not a creature called Odradek. At first glance it looks like a flat star-shaped spool for thread, and indeed it does seem to have thread wound upon it; to be sure, they are only old, broken-off bits of thread, knotted and tangled together, of the most varied sorts and colors. But it is not only a spool, for a small wooden crossbar sticks out of the middle of the star, and another small rod is joined to that at a right angle. By means of this latter rod on one side and one of the points of the star on the other, the whole thing can stand upright as if on two legs.

Is Odradek a "thing," as the bemused family man begins by calling him, or is he not a childlike creature, a daemon at home in the world of children? Odradek clearly was made by an inventive and humorous child, rather in the spirit of the making of Adam out of the moistened red clay by the J writer's Yahweh. It is difficult not to read Odradek's creation as a deliberate parody, when we are told that "the whole thing can stand upright as if on two legs," and again when the suggestion is ventured that Odradek, like Adam, "once had some sort of intelligible shape and is now only a broken-down remnant." If Odradek is fallen, he is still quite jaunty, and cannot be closely scrutinized, since he "is extraordinarily nimble and can never be laid hold of," like the story in which he appears. Odradek not only advises you not to do anything about him, but in some clear sense he is yet another figure by means of whom Kafka advises you against interpreting Kafka.

One of the loveliest moments in all of Kafka comes when you, the paterfamilias, encounter Odradek leaning directly beneath you against the banisters. Being inclined to speak to him, as you would to a child, you receive a surprise:

> "Well, what's your name?" you ask him. "Odradek," he says. "And where do you live?" "No fixed abode," he says and laughs; but it is only the kind of laughter that has no lungs behind it. It sounds rather like the rustling of fallen leaves.

"The 'I' is another," Rimbaud once wrote, adding: "So much the worse for the wood that finds it is a violin." So much the worse for the wood that finds it is Odradek. He laughs at being a vagrant, if only by the bourgeois definition of having "no fixed abode," but the laughter, not being human, is uncanny. And so he provokes the family man to an uncanny reflection, which may be a Kafkan parody of Freud's death drive beyond the pleasure principle:

> I ask myself, to no purpose, what is likely to happen to him? Can he possibly die? Anything that dies has had some kind of aim in life, some kind of activity, which has worn out; but that does not apply to Odradek. Am I to suppose, then, that he will always be rolling down the stairs, with ends of thread trailing after him, right before the feet of my children? He does no harm to anything that I can see, but the idea that he is likely to survive me I find almost painful.

The aim of life, Freud says, is death, is the return of the organic to the inorganic, supposedly our earlier state of being. Our activity wears out, and so we die because, in an uncanny sense, we wish to die. But Odradek, harmless and charming, is a child's creation, aimless, and so not subject to the death drive. Odradek is immortal, being daemonic, and he represents also a Freudian return of the repressed, while (even as) a complete affective repression is maintained. The family man introjects Odradek intellectually, but totally projects him affectively. Odradek, I now suggest, is best understood as Kafka's synecdoche for *Verneinung*, Kafka's version (not altogether un-Freudian) of Jewish negation.

Why does Kafka have so unique a spiritual authority? Perhaps the question should be rephrased. What kind of spiritual authority does Kafka have for us, or why are we moved or compelled to read him as one who has such authority? Why invoke the question of authority at all? Literary authority, however we define it, has no necessary relation to spiritual authority, and to speak of a spiritual authority in Jewish writing anyway always has been to speak rather dubiously. Authority is not a Jewish concept but a Roman one, and so makes perfect contemporary sense in the context of the Roman Catholic Church but little sense in Jewish matters, despite the squalors of Israeli politics and the flaccid pieties of American Jewish nostalgias. There is no authority without hierarchy, and hierarchy is not a very Jewish concept either. We do not want the rabbis, or anyone else, to tell us what or who is or is not Jewish. The masks of the normative conceal not only the eclecticism of Judaism and of Jewish culture, but also the nature of the J writer's Yahweh himself. It is absurd to think of Yahweh as having mere authority. He is no Roman godling who augments human activities, nor a Homeric god helping to constitute an audience for human heroism.

Yahweh is neither a founder nor an onlooker, though sometimes he can be mistaken for either or both. His essential trope is fatherhood rather than foundation, and his interventions are those of a covenanter rather than a spectator. You cannot found an authority upon him, because his benignity is manifested not through augmentation but through creation. He does not write; he speaks, and he is heard, in time, and what he continues to create by his speaking is *olam,* time without boundaries, which is more than just an augmentation. More of anything else can come through authority, but more life is the blessing itself, and comes, beyond authority, to Abraham, to Jacob, and to David. No more than Yahweh do any of them have mere authority. Yet Kafka certainly does have literary authority, and in a troubled way his literary authority is now spiritual also, particularly in Jewish contexts. I do not think that this is a post-Holocaust phenomenon, though Jewish Gnosticism, oxymoronic as it may or may not be, certainly seems appropriate to our time to many among us. Literary Gnosticism does not seem to me a time-bound phenomenon, anyway. Kafka's *The Castle,* as Erich Heller has agreed, is clearly more Gnostic than normative in its spiritual temper, but then so is Shakespeare's *Macbeth,* and Blake's *The Four Zoas,* and Carlyle's *Sartor Resartus.* We sense a Jewish element in Kafka's apparent Gnosticism, even if we are less prepared than Scholem was to name it as a new Kabbalah. In his 1922 diaries, Kafka subtly insinuated that even his espousal of the negative was dialectical:

> The Negative alone, however strong it may be, cannot suffice, as in my unhappiest moments I believe it can. For if I have gone the tiniest step upward, won any, be it the most dubious kind of security for myself, I then stretch out on my step and wait for the Negative, not to climb up to me, indeed, but to drag me down from it. Hence it is a defensive instinct in me that won't tolerate my having the slightest degree of lasting ease and smashes the marriage bed, for example, even before it has been set up.

What is the Kafkan negative, whether in this passage or elsewhere? Let us begin by dismissing the Gallic notion that there is anything Hegelian about it, any more than there is anything Hegelian about the Freudian *Verneinung*. Kafka's negative, unlike Freud's, is uneasily and remotely descended from the ancient tradition of negative theology, and perhaps even from that most negative of ancient theologies, Gnosticism, and yet Kafka, despite his yearnings for transcendence, joins Freud in accepting the ultimate authority of the fact. The given suffers no destruction in Kafka or in Freud, and this given essentially is the way things are, for everyone, and for the Jews in particular. If fact is supreme, then, the mediation of the Hegelian negative becomes an absurdity, and no destructive use of such a negative is possible, which is to say that Heidegger becomes impossible, and Derrida, who is a strong misreading of Heidegger, becomes quite unnecessary.

The Kafkan negative most simply is his Judaism, which is to say the spiritual form of Kafka's self-conscious Jewishness, as exemplified in that extraordinary aphorism: "What is laid upon us is to accomplish the negative; the positive is already given." The positive here is the Law or normative Judaism; the negative is not so much Kafka's new Kabbalah as it is that which is still laid upon us: the Judaism of the negative, of the future as it is always rushing toward us.

His best biographer to date, Ernst Pawel, emphasizes Kafka's consciousness "of his identity as a Jew, not in the religious, but in the national sense." Still, Kafka was not a Zionist, and perhaps he longed not so much for Zion as for a Jewish language, be it Yiddish or Hebrew. He could not see that his astonishing stylistic purity in German was precisely his way of *not* betraying his self-identity as a Jew. In his final phase, Kafka thought of going to Jerusalem, and again intensified his study of Hebrew. Had he lived, he would probably have gone to Zion, perfected a vernacular Hebrew, and given us the bewilderment of Kafkan parables and stories in the language of the J writer and of Judah Halevi.

What calls out for interpretation in Kafka is his refusal to be interpreted, his evasiveness even in the realm of his own negative. Two of his most beautifully enigmatical performances, both late, are the parable "The Problem of Our Laws" and the story or testament "Josephine the Singer, or the Mouse Folk." Each allows a cognitive return of Jewish cultural memory, while refusing the affective identification that would make either work specifically Jewish in either historical or contemporary identification. "The Problem of Our Laws" is set as a problem in the parable's first paragraph:

> Our laws are not generally known; they are kept secret by the small group of nobles who rule us. We are convinced that these ancient laws are scrupulously administered; nevertheless it is an extremely painful thing to be ruled by laws that one does not know. I am not thinking of possible discrepancies that may arise in the interpretation of the laws, or of the disadvantages involved when only a few and not the whole people are allowed to have a say in their interpretation. These disadvantages are perhaps of no great importance. For the laws are very ancient; their interpretation has been the work of centuries, and has itself doubtless acquired the status of law; and though there is still a possible freedom of interpretation left, it has now become very restricted. Moreover the nobles have obviously no cause to be influenced in their interpretation by personal interests inimical to us, for the laws were made to the advantage of the nobles from the very beginning, they themselves stand above the laws, and that seems to be why the laws were entrusted exclusively into their hands. Of course, there is wisdom in that—who doubts the wisdom of the ancient laws?—but also hardship for us; probably that is unavoidable.

In Judaism, the Law is precisely what is generally known, proclaimed and taught by the normative sages. The Kabbalah was secret doctrine, but increasingly was guarded not by the normative rabbis, but by Gnostic sectaries, Sabbatians and Frankists, all of them ideologically descended from Nathan of Gaza, Sabbatai Zevi's prophet. Kafka twists askew the relation between normative and esoteric Judaism, again making a synecdochal representation impossible. It is not the rabbis or normative sages who stand above the Torah but the *minim,* the heretics from Elisha Ben Abuyah through to Jacob Frank, and in some sense, Gershom Scholem as well. To these Jewish Gnostics, as the parable goes on to insinuate, "The Law is whatever the nobles do." So radical a definition tells us that "the tradition is far from complete," and that a kind of messianic expectation is therefore necessary.

> This view, so comfortless as far as the present is concerned, is lightened only by the belief that a time will eventually come when the tradition and our research into it will jointly reach their conclusion, and as it were gain a breathing space, when everything will become clear, the law will belong to the people, and the nobility will vanish.

If the parable at this point were to be translated into early Christian terms, then the nobility would be the Pharisees, and the people would be the Christian believers. But Kafka moves rapidly to stop such a translation:

> This is not maintained in any spirit of hatred against the nobility; not at all, and by no one. We are more inclined to hate ourselves, because we have not yet shown ourselves worthy of being entrusted with the laws.

"We" here cannot be either Christians or Jews. Who then are those who have not yet shown themselves "worthy of being entrusted with the laws?" They would appear to be the crows or jackdaws again, a Kafka or a Hunter Gracchus, wandering about in a state perhaps vulnerable to self-hatred or self-distrust, waiting for a Torah that will not be revealed. Audaciously, Kafka then concludes with overt paradox:

> Actually one can express the problem only in a sort of paradox: Any party that would repudiate not only all belief in the laws, but the nobility as well, would have the whole people behind it; yet no such party can come into existence, for nobody would dare to repudiate the nobility. We live on this razor's edge. A writer once summed the matter up in this way: The sole visible and indubitable law that is imposed upon us is the nobility, and must we ourselves deprive ourselves of that one law?

Why would no one dare to repudiate the nobility, whether we read them as normative Pharisees, Jewish Gnostic heresiarchs, or whatever? Though imposed upon us, the sages or the *minim* are the only visible evidence of law that we have. Who are we then? How is the parable's final question, whether open or rhetorical, to be answered? "Must we ourselves deprive ourselves of that one law?" Blake's answer, in *The Marriage of Heaven and Hell*, was "One Law for the Lion & Ox is Oppression." But what is one law for the crows? Kafka will not tell us whether it is oppression or not.

Josephine the singer also is a crow or *kafka*, rather than a mouse, and the folk may be interpreted as an entire nation of jackdaws. The spirit of the Negative, dominant if uneasy in "The Problem of Our Laws," is loosed into a terrible freedom in Kafka's testamentary story. That is to say: in the parable, the laws could not be Torah, though that analogue flickered near. But in Josephine's story, the mouse folk simultaneously are and are not the Jewish people, and Franz Kafka both is and is not their curious singer. Cognitively the identifications are possible, as though returned from forgetfulness, but affectively they certainly are not, unless we can assume that crucial aspects making up the identifications have been purposefully, if other than consciously, forgotten. Josephine's piping *is* Kafka's story, and yet Kafka's story is hardly Josephine's piping.

Can there be a mode of negation neither conscious nor unconscious, neither Hegelian nor Freudian? Kafka's genius provides one, exposing many shades between consciousness and the work of repression, many demarcations far ghostlier than we could have imagined without him. Perhaps the ghostliest come at the end of the story:

> Josephine's road, however, must go downhill. The time will soon come when her last notes sound and die into silence. She is a small episode in the eternal history of our people, and the people will get over the loss of her. Not that it will be easy for us; how can our gatherings take place in utter silence? Still, were they not silent even when Josephine was present? Was her actual piping notably louder and more alive than the memory of it will be? Was it even in her lifetime more than a simple memory? Was it not rather because Josephine's singing was already past losing in this way that our people in their wisdom prized it so highly?
>
> So perhaps we shall not miss so very much after all, while Josephine, redeemed from the earthly sorrows which to her thinking lay in wait for all chosen spirits, will happily lose herself in the numberless throng of the heroes of our people, and soon, since we are no historians, will rise to the heights of redemption and be forgotten like all her brothers.

"I am a Memory come alive," Kafka wrote in the diaries. Whether or not he intended it, he was Jewish memory come alive. "Was it even in her lifetime more than a simple memory?" Kafka asks, knowing that he too was past losing. The Jews are no historians, in some sense, because Jewish memory, as Yosef Yerushalmi has demonstrated, is a normative mode and not a historical one. Kafka, if he could have prayed, might have prayed to rise to the heights of redemption and be forgotten like most of his brothers and sisters. But his prayer would not have been answered. When we think of *the* Catholic writer, we think of Dante, who nevertheless had the audacity to enshrine his Beatrice in the hierarchy of Paradise. If we think of *the* Protestant writer, we think of Milton, a party or sect of one, who believed that the soul was mortal, and would be resurrected only in conjunction with the body. Think of *the* Jewish writer, and you must think of Kafka, who evaded his own audacity, and believed nothing, and trusted only in the covenant of being a writer.

やぶ

Kafka always feared that he would perish of the truth, of the only truth he knew, which was to trust in his covenant as a writer. What can it mean to trust in the covenant, not between Yahweh and the Jewish people but between writing and a writer? Gregor Samsa is a solitary (his last name can be translated from Czech as "I am alone"), a commercial traveler, and a kind of family pariah or outcast, at least in his own tormented vision. His celebrated metamorphosis into a kind of huge bedbug is completed in the story's first sentence. Gregor's fate is certain but without hope; there is plenty of hope, for writing as for God, but none for Gregor. The law, which is the way things are, including one's parents' huge debt to one's employer, is essentially a universal compulsion to repeat. No irony, however well handled, can represent repetition compulsion as the Law of the Jews. Samsa's employer is therefore not Yahweh but another version of the Gnostic Demiurge, ruler of the cosmological emptiness in which we dwell.

The only rage to order that Kafka knew was his implicit rage not to be interpreted. There can be no ultimate coherence to my Gnostic interpretation (nor to Scholem's, nor Benjamin's, nor Heller's, nor to anyone's) because Kafka refuses the Gnostic quest for the alien God, for one's own spark or *pneuma* rejoining the original abyss somewhere out of this world. The huge bedbug is neither the fallen husk of Samsa nor his potentially saving *pneuma*. It can hardly be his spark from the original abyss because it is a horrible vermin, and yet only after his transformation into a bug is Gregor capable of aesthetic apprehension. Like Shakespeare's grotesque Caliban, the insect Samsa hears the beautiful in music, and so for the first time apprehends another sphere. Kafka refused an illustration for *The Metamorphosis* that would have portrayed Gregor Samsa as a literal beetle or bedbug: "The insect itself cannot be drawn. It cannot be drawn even as if seen from a distance." This is not to say that Samsa suffers a hallucination; it only reminds us that a negation cannot be visually represented, which in turn reminds us of Kafkan nostalgias for the Second Commandment.

Is Gregor accurate in his final perception that his death is a liberation, an act of love for his family? Wilhelm Emrich, elsewhere so wary a Kafka exegete, fell into this momentary passion for the positive, an entrapment all readers of Kafka suffer sooner or later, so exhausted are we by this greatest master of evasions. Because the insect is inexplicable, it does not necessarily contain any truth. *The Metamorphosis*, like all crucial Kafkan narratives, takes place somewhere *between* truth and meaning, a "somewhere" identical with the modern Jewish rupture from the normative tradition. Truth is in hope and neither is available to us, while meaning is in the future or the messianic age, and we will not attain either. We are lazy, but industry will not avail us either, not even the industrial zeal with which every writer prides himself upon accepting his own death. If *The Metamorphosis* is a satire, then it is self-satire, or post-Nietzschean parody, that humiliates Kafka's only covenant, the placing of trust in the transcendental possibility of being a strong writer.

The story then cannot be interpreted coherently as a fantasy of death and resurrection, or as an allegory on the less-is-more

fate of being a writer. Gregor's death is not an effectual sacrifice, not a self-fulfillment, and not even a tragic irony of any
kind. It is another Kafkan negation that refuses to negate the
given, which is the world of Freud's reality principle. Gregor
does not become a child again as he dies. Yet we cannot even
call him a failure, which might guarantee his upward fall to the
heights of redemption. Like Gracchus, like the bucket-rider,
like the country doctor, like the hunger artist, Gregor is sus-
pended between the truth of the past, or Jewish memory, and
the meaning of the future, or Jewish messianism. Poor Gregor
therefore evades the categories both of belief and of poetry.
How much would most of us know about this rupture without Kafka, or Kafka's true heir, Beckett?

A Gnosticism without transcendence is not a knowing but is
something else, and there is no transcendence in *The Metamorphosis,* or anywhere in Kafka. To transcend in a world of
rupture you only need to change your direction, but that is to
adopt the stance of the cat (or Gnostic Archon) of Kafka's
magnificent and appalling parable, "A Little Fable":

> "Alas," said the mouse, "the world is growing smaller every day.
> At the beginning it was so big that I was afraid. I kept running
> and running, and I was glad when at last I saw walls far away
> to the right and left, but these long walls have narrowed so
> quickly that I am in the last chamber already, and there in the
> corner stands the trap that I must run into." "You only need to
> change your direction," said the cat, and ate it up.

"Guilt" generally seems more a Christian than a Jewish cate-
gory, even if the guilt of Joseph K. is primarily ignorance of
the Law. Certainly Kafka could be judged closer to Freud in
The Trial than he usually is, since Freudian guilt is also hardly
distinct from ignorance, not of the Law but of the reality principle. Freud insisted that all authority, communal or personal,

induced guilt in us, since we share in the murder of the totemic father. Guilt therefore is never to be doubted, but only because we are all of us more or less ill, all plagued by our discomfort with culture. Freudian and Kafkan guilt alike are known only under the sign of negation, rather than as emotion. Joseph K. has no consciousness of having done wrong, but just as Freudian man nurtures the desire to destroy authority or the father, so even Joseph K. has his own unfulfilled wishes against the image of the Law.

The process that Joseph K. undergoes is hopeless, since the Law is essentially a closed Kabbalah; its books are not available to the accused. If traditional questers suffered an ordeal by landscape, Joseph K.'s ordeal is by nearly everything and everyone he encounters. The representatives of the Law, and their camp followers, are so unsavory that Joseph K. seems sympathetic by contrast, yet he is actually a poor fellow in himself, and would be as nasty as the keepers of the Law, if only he could. *The Trial* is a very unpleasant book, and Kafka's own judgment of it may have been spiritually wiser than the enunciations of its critics. Would there be any process for us to undergo if we were not both lazy and frightened? Nietzsche's motive for metaphor was the desire to be different, the desire to be elsewhere, but Kafka's sense of our motive is that we want to rest, even if just for a moment. The world is our Gnostic catastrophe creation, broken into existence by the guilt of our repose. Yet this is creation, and can be visibly beautiful, even as the accused are beautiful in the gaze of the camp followers of the Law.

I do not think that the process Joseph K. undergoes can be called "interpretation," which is the judgment of Ernst Pawel, who follows Jewish tradition in supposing that the Law is language. *The Trial,* like the rest of Kafka's writings, is a parable not of interpretation but of the necessary failure of interpretation. I would surmise that the Law is not all of language, since

the language of *The Trial* is ironic enough to suggest that it is
not altogether bound to the Law. If *The Trial* has a center, it is
in what Kafka thought worthy of publishing: the famous parable "Before the Law." The dialogue concerning the parable
between Joseph K. and the prison chaplain who tells it is remarkable, but less crucial than the parable itself:

> Before the Law stands a doorkeeper on guard. To this door-
> keeper there comes a man from the country who begs for ad-
> mittance to the Law. But the doorkeeper says that he cannot
> admit the man at the moment. The man, on reflection, asks if
> he will be allowed, then, to enter later. "It is possible," answers
> the doorkeeper, "but not at this moment." Since the door lead-
> ing into the Law stands open as usual and the doorkeeper steps
> to one side, the man bends down to peer through the entrance.
> When the doorkeeper sees that, he laughs and says: "If you are
> so strongly tempted, try to get in without my permission. But
> note that I am powerful. And I am only the lowest doorkeeper.
> From hall to hall keepers stand at every door, one more power-
> ful than the other. Even the third of these has an aspect that
> even I cannot bear to look at." These are difficulties which the
> man from the country has not expected to meet, the Law, he
> thinks, should be accessible to every man and at all times, but
> when he looks more closely at the doorkeeper in his furred
> robe, with his huge pointed nose and long, thin, Tartar beard,
> he decides that he had better wait until he gets permission to
> enter. The doorkeeper gives him a stool and lets him sit down at
> the side of the door. There he sits waiting for days and years.
> He makes many attempts to be allowed in and wearies the door-
> keeper with his importunity. The doorkeeper often engages
> him in brief conversation, asking him about his home and
> about other matters, but the questions are put quite imper-
> sonally, as great men put questions, and always conclude with
> the statement that the man cannot be allowed to enter yet.
> The man, who has equipped himself with many things for his
> journey, parts with all he has, however valuable, in the hope of
> bribing the doorkeeper. The doorkeeper accepts it all, saying,
> however, as he takes each gift: "I take this only to keep you

from feeling that you have left something undone." During all these long years the man watches the doorkeeper almost incessantly. He forgets about the other doorkeepers, and this one seems to him the only barrier between himself and the Law. In the first years he curses his evil fate aloud; later, as he grows old, he only mutters to himself. He grows childish, and since in his prolonged watch he has learned to know even the fleas in the doorkeeper's fur collar, he begs the very fleas to help him and to persuade the doorkeeper to change his mind. Finally his eyes grow dim and he does not know whether the world is really darkening around him or whether his eyes are only deceiving him. But in the darkness he can now perceive a radiance that streams immortally from the door of the Law. Now his life is drawing to a close. Before he dies, all that he has experienced during the whole time of his sojourn condenses in his mind into one question, which he has never yet put to the doorkeeper. He beckons the doorkeeper, since he can no longer raise his stiffening body. The doorkeeper has to bend far down to hear him, for the difference in size between them has increased very much to the man's disadvantage. "What do you want to know now?" asks the doorkeeper, "you are insatiable." "Everyone strives to attain the Law," answers the man, "how does it come about, then, that in all these years no one has come seeking admittance but me?" The doorkeeper perceives that the man is at the end of his strength and that his hearing is failing, so he bellows in his ear: "No one but you could gain admittance through this door, since this door was intended only for you. I am now going to shut it."

Does he actually perceive a radiance, or are his eyes perhaps still deceiving him? What would admittance to the radiance mean? The Law, I take it, has the same status it has in the later parable, "The Problem of Our Laws," where it cannot be Torah, or the Jewish Law, yet Torah flickers uneasily near as a positive analogue to the negation that is playing itself out. Joseph K. then is another jackdaw, another Kafkan crow in a cosmos of crows, waiting for that new Torah that will not be revealed. Does such a waiting allow itself to be represented in or by a novel? No one could judge *The Trial* to be grander as a whole than in its parts, and "Before the Law" bursts out of its narrative shell in the novel. The terrible greatness of Kafka is absolute in the parable, but wavering in the novel, too impure a casing for such a fire.

That there should be nothing but a spiritual world, Kafka once wrote, denies us hope but gives us certainty. The certainty would seem to be not so much that a radiance exists, but that all access to it will be barred by petty officials at least countenanced, if not encouraged, by what passes for the radiance itself. This is not paradox, any more than is the Kafkan principle propounded by the priest who narrates "Before the Law": accurate interpretation and misreading cannot altogether exclude one another. Kafka's aesthetic compulsion (can there be such?) in *The Trial* as elsewhere is to write so as to create a necessity, yet also so as to make interpretation impossible rather than merely difficult.

Kafka's permanent centrality to the postnormative Jewish dilemma is confirmed in *The Trial*. Gershom Scholem found in Kafka not only the true continuator of the Gnostic Kabbalah of Moses Cordovero but also the central representative for our time of an even more archaic splendor, the broken radiance of Hebraic revelation. Perhaps Scholem was right, for no other modern Jewish author troubles us with so strong an impression that we are in the presence of what Scholem called "the strong light of the canonical, of the perfection that destroys."

The full-scale instance of Kafka's new negative or new Kabbalah is *The Castle,* an unfinished and unfinishable autobiographical novel, which is the story of K., the land surveyor. What is written between its lines? Assaulting the last earthly frontier, K. is necessarily audacious, but if what lies beyond the frontier is represented ultimately by Klamm, who is an imprisoning silence and is lord of the *kenoma* or cosmic emptiness, then no audacity can suffice. You cannot redraw the frontiers, even if the authorities desire it, when you arrive at the administrative center of a catastrophe creation, where the demarcations hold fast against a supposed chaos or abyss, which is actually the negative emblem of the truth that the false or marred creation refuses. *The Castle* is the tale of how Kafka cannot write his way back to the abyss, of how K. cannot do his work as land surveyor.

Part of K.'s burden is that he is not audacious enough, even though audacity could not be enough anyway. Here is the interpretive audacity of Erich Heller, in *Franz Kafka,* rightly rejecting all those who identify the Castle with spirituality and authentic grace, but himself missing the ineluctable evasiveness of Kafka's new Kabbalah:

> The Castle of Kafka's novel is, as it were, the heavily fortified garrison of a company of Gnostic demons, successfully holding an advanced position against the maneuvers of an impatient soul. There is no conceivable idea of divinity which could justify those interpreters who see in the Castle the residence of "divine law and divine grace." Its officers are totally indifferent to good if they are not positively wicked. Neither in their decrees nor in their activities is there any trace of love, mercy, charity, or majesty. In their icy detachment they inspire certainly no awe, but fear and revulsion. Their servants are a plague to the village, "a wild, unmanageable lot, ruled by their insatiable impulses . . . their scandalous behavior knows no limits," an anticipation of the blackguards who were to become the footmen of European dictators rather than the office boys of a divine ministry. Compared to the petty and apparently calculated torture of this tyranny, the gods of Shakespeare's indignation who "kill us for their sport" are at least majestic in their wantonness.

On such a reading, Klamm would be the Demiurge, leader of a company of Archons, gods of this world. Kafka is too evasive and too negative to give us so positive and simplistic an account of triumphant evil, or at least of reigning indifference to the good. Such Gnostic symbolism would make Klamm and his cohorts representatives of ignorance, and K. in contrast a knower, but K. knows almost nothing, particularly about his own self, and from the start overestimates his own strength, even as he deceives himself into the belief that the Castle underestimates him. The Castle is there primarily because K. is ignorant, though K.'s deepest drive is for knowledge. K.'s largest error throughout is his desire for a personal confrontation with Klamm, which necessarily is impossible. K., the single crow or jackdaw, would be sufficient to destroy the authority of Klamm, but Klamm and the Castle of Westwest signify simply the absence of crows, the inability of K. to achieve knowledge, and therefore the impossibility of K. himself, the failure of land surveying or of assaulting the frontiers, of writing a new Kabbalah.

Klamm is named by Wilhelm Emrich as the interpersonal element in the erotic, which seems to me just as subtle an error as judging Klamm to be the Demiurge, leader of a company of Gnostic demons. It might be more accurate to call Klamm the impersonal element in the erotic, the drive, as Martin Greenberg does, yet even that identification is evaded by Kafka's text. Closer to Klamm, as should be expected, is the negative aspect of the drive, its entropy, whose effect upon consciousness is nihilistic. Freud, in his posthumous *Outline of Psychoanalysis* (1940) says of the drives that "they represent the somatic demands upon mental life." That approximates Klamm, but only if you give priority to Thanatos over Eros, to the death drive over sexuality. Wilhelm Emrich, a touch humorlessly, even identifies Klamm with Eros in his *Franz Kafka,* which would give us a weird Eros indeed:

> Accordingly, then, Klamm is the "power" that brings the lovers together as well as the power which, bestowing happiness and

bliss, is present within love itself. K. seeks contact with this power, sensing its proximity in love, a proximity great enough for communicating in whispers; but he must "manifest" such communication and contact with this power itself through a spiritual-intellectual expression of his own; this means that, as an independent spiritual-intellectual being, he must confront this power eye to eye, as it were: he must "manifest" to this super-personal power his own understanding, his own relation with it, a relation "known" only to him at the present time; that means, he must make this relation known to the power as well.

Emrich seems to found this equation on the love affair between K. and Frieda, which begins, in famous squalor, on the floor of a bar:

Fortunately Frieda soon came back; she did not mention K., she only complained about the peasants, and in the course of looking round for K. went behind the counter, so that he was able to touch her foot. From that moment he felt safe. Since Frieda made no reference to K., however, the landlord was compelled to do it. "And where is the Land-Surveyor?" he asked. He was probably courteous by nature, refined by constant and relatively free intercourse with men who were much his superior, but there was remarkable consideration in his tone to Frieda, which was all the more striking because in his conversation he did not cease to be an employer addressing a servant, and a saucy servant at that. "The Land-Surveyor—I forgot all about him," said Frieda, setting her small foot on K.'s chest. "He must have gone out long ago." "But I haven't seen him," said the landlord, "and I was in the hall nearly the whole time." "Well, he isn't in here," said Frieda coolly. "Perhaps he's hidden somewhere," said the landlord. "From the impression I had of him, he's capable of a good deal." "He would hardly dare to do that," said Frieda, pressing her foot down on K. There was a certain mirth and freedom about her which K. had not previously noticed, and quite unexpectedly it took the upper hand, for suddenly laughing she bent down to K. with the words: "Perhaps he's hidden underneath here," kissed him lightly, and sprang up again saying with a troubled air: "No, he's not there." Then the landlord, too, surprised K. when he said: "It bothers me not to know for certain that he's gone. Not only because of Herr Klamm, but because of the rule of the house. And the rules applies to you, Fräulein Frieda, just as much as to me. Well, if you answer for the bar, I'll go through the rest of the rooms. Good night! Sleep well!" He could hardly have left the room before Frieda had turned out the electric light and was under the counter beside K. "My darling! My darling!" she whispered, but she did not touch him. As if swooning with love, she lay on her back and stretched out her arms; time must have seemed endless to her in the prospect of her happiness, and she sighed rather than sang some little song or other. Then as K. still lay absorbed in thought, she started up and began to tug at him like a child. "Come on, it's too close down here," and they embraced each other, her little body burned in K.'s hands, in a state of unconsciousness which K. tried again and again but in vain to master they rolled a little way, landing with a thud on Klamm's door, where they lay among the small puddles of beer and other refuse scattered on the floor.

"Landing with a thud on Klamm's door" is Kafka's outrageously rancid trope for a successful completion to copulation, but that hardly makes Klamm into a benign Eros, with his devotees lying "among the small puddles of beer and other refuse scattered on the floor." One could recall the libertines among the Gnostics, ancient and modern, who seek to redeem the sparks upward by a redemption *through* sin. Frieda, faithful disciple and former mistress of Klamm, tells K. that she believes it is Klamm's "doing that we came together there under the counter; blessed, not cursed, be the hour." Emrich gives full credence to Frieda, a rather dangerous act for an exegete, and certainly K. desperately believes Frieda, but then, as Heller remarks, "K. loves Frieda—if he loves her at all—entirely for Klamm's sake." That K., despite his drive for freedom, may be deceived as to Klamm's nature is understandable, but I do not think that Kafka was deceived, or wished to be deceived. If Klamm is to be identified, it ought to be with what is silent, imprisoned, and unavailable in copulation, something that partakes of the final negative, the drive toward death.

Whether *The Castle* is of the aesthetic eminence of Kafka's finest stories, parables, and fragments is open to considerable doubt, but *The Castle* is certainly the best text for studying Kafka's negative, his hidden and subversive new Kabbalah. It abides as the most enigmatic major novel of our century, and one sees why Kafka himself thought it a failure. But all Kabbalah—old and new—has to fail when it offers itself openly to more than a handful. Perhaps *The Castle* fails as the *Zohar* fails, but like the *Zohar*, Kafka's *Castle* will go on failing from one era to another.

Jonathan Swift, the strongest ironist in English, wrote the prose masterpiece of the language in *A Tale of a Tub*. Samuel Beckett, as much the legitimate descendant of Swift as he is of his friend James Joyce, has written the prose masterpieces of the language in this century, sometimes as translations from his own French originals. Such an assertion does not discount the baroque splendors of *Ulysses* and *Finnegans Wake* but prefers to them the purity of *Murphy* and *Watt,* and of Beckett's renderings into English of *Malone Dies, The Unnameable,* and *How It Is.* Unlike Swift and Joyce, Beckett is only secondarily an ironist and, despite his brilliance at tragicomedy, is something other than a comic writer. His Cartesian dualism seems to me less fundamental than his profoundly Schopenhauerian vision. Perhaps Swift, had he read and tolerated Schopenhauer, might have turned into Beckett.

A remarkable number of the greatest novelists have found Schopenhauer more than congenial: one thinks of Turgenev, Tolstoy, Zola, Hardy, Conrad, Thomas Mann, even of Proust.

As those seven novelists have in common only the activity of writing novels, we may suspect that Schopenhauer's really horrifying system helps a novelist to do his work. This is not to discount the intellectual and spiritual persuasiveness of Schopenhauer. A philosopher who so deeply affected Wagner, Nietzsche, Wittgenstein, and (despite his denials) Freud can hardly be regarded only as a convenient aid to storytellers and storytelling. Nevertheless, Schopenhauer evidently stimulated the arts of fiction, but why? Certain it is that we cannot read *The World as Will and Representation* as a work of fiction. Who could bear it as fiction? Supplementing his book, Schopenhauer characterizes the will to live:

> Here also life presents itself by no means as a gift for enjoyment, but as a task, a drudgery to be performed; and in accordance with this we see, in great and small, universal need, ceaseless cares, constant pressure, endless strife, compulsory activity, with extreme exertion of all the powers of body and mind . . . All strive, some planning, others acting; the tumult is indescribable. But the ultimate aim of it all, what is it? To sustain ephemeral and tormented individuals through a short span of time in the most fortunate case with endurable want and comparative freedom from pain, which, however, is at once attended with ennui; then the reproduction of this race and its striving. In this evident disproportion between the trouble and the reward, the will to live appears to us from this point of view, if taken objectively, as a fool, or subjectively, as a delusion, seized by which everything living works with the utmost exertion of its strength for something that is of no value. But when we consider it more closely, we shall find here also that it is rather a blind pressure, a tendency entirely without ground or motive.

Hugh Kenner suggests that Beckett reads Descartes as fiction. Beckett's fiction suggests that Beckett reads Schopenhauer as truth. Descartes as a precursor is safely distant; Joyce was much too close, and *Murphy* and even *Watt* are Joycean books. Doubtless, Beckett turned to French in *Molloy* so as to exorcise Joyce, and certainly, from *Malone Dies* on, the prose when translated back into English has ceased to be Joycean. Joyce is to Beckett as Milton was to Wordsworth. *Finnegans Wake,* like *Paradise Lost,* is a triumph demanding study; Beckett's trilogy, like *The Prelude,* internalizes the triumph by way of the compensatory imagination, in which experience and loss become one. Study does little to unriddle Beckett, or Wordsworth. The Old Cumberland Beggar, Michael, Margaret of *The Ruined Cottage*: these resist analysis as do Molloy, Malone, the Unnameable. Place my namesake, the sublime Poldy, in *Murphy* and he might fit, though he would explode the book. Place him in *Watt*? It cannot be done, and Poldy (or even Earwicker) in the trilogy would be like Milton (or Satan) perambulating about in *The Prelude.*

The fashion (largely derived from French misreaders of German thought) of denying a fixed, stable ego is a shibboleth of current criticism. But such a denial is precisely like each literary generation's assertion that it truly writes the common language rather than a poetic diction. Both stances define modernism, and modernism is as old as Hellenistic Alexandria. Callimachus is as modernist as Joyce, and Aristarchus, like Hugh Kenner, is an antiquarian modernist or modernist antiquarian. Schopenhauer dismissed the ego as an illusion, life as torment, and the universe as nothing, and he rightly credited these insights to that great modernist, the Buddha. Beckett too is as modernist as the Buddha, or as Schopenhauer, who disputes with Hume the position of the best writer among philosophers since Plato. I laugh sometimes in reading Schopenhauer, but the laughter is defensive. Beckett provokes laughter, as Falstaff does, or in the mode of Shakespeare's clowns.

ë&

In his early monograph, *Proust,* Beckett cites Schopenhauer's definition of the artistic procedure as "the contemplation of the world independently of the principle of reason." Such more-than-rational contemplation gives Proust those Ruskinian or Paterian privileged moments that are "epiphanies" in Joyce but which Beckett mordantly calls "fetishes" in Proust. Transcendental bursts of radiance necessarily are no part of Beckett's cosmos, which resembles, if anything at all, the Demiurge's creation in ancient Gnosticism. Basilides or Valentinus, Alexandrian heresiarchs, would have recognized instantly the world of the trilogy and of the major plays: *Waiting for Godot, Endgame, Krapp's Last Tape.* It is the world ruled by the Archons, the *kenoma,* nonplace of emptiness. Beckett's enigmatic spirituality quests (though sporadically) for a void that is a fullness, the abyss or *pleroma* that the Gnostics named both forefather and foremother. Call this a natural rather than a revealed Gnosticism in Beckett's case, but Gnosticism it is nevertheless. Schopenhauer's quietism is at last not Beckett's, which is to say that for Beckett, as for Blake and for the gnostics, the Creation and the Fall were the same event.

The young Beckett, bitterly reviewing a translation of Rilke into English, memorably rejected Rilke's transcendental self-deceptions, where the poet mistook his own tropes as spiritual evidences: "Such a turmoil of self-deception and naif discontent gains nothing in dignity from that prime article of the Rilkean faith, which provides for the interchangeability of Rilke and God . . . He has the fidgets, a disorder which may very well give rise, as it did with Rilke on occasion, to poetry of a high order. But why call the fidgets God, Ego, Orpheus and the rest?"

In 1938, the year that *Murphy* was belatedly published, Beckett declared his double impatience, with the language of transcendence and the transcendence of language, while intimating also the imminence of the swerve away from Joyce in the composition of *Watt* (1942–1944):

> At first it can only be a matter of somehow finding a method by which we can represent this mocking attitude towards the word, through words. In this dissonance between the means and their use it will perhaps become possible to feel a whisper of that final music or that silence that underlies All.
>
> With such a program, in my opinion, the latest work of Joyce has nothing whatever to do. There it seems rather to be a matter of an apotheosis of the word. Unless perhaps Ascension to Heaven and Descent to Hell are somehow one and the same.

The way of a Gnostic imagination is descent, in what cannot be called a hope to liberate the sparks imprisoned in words. Hope is alien to Beckett's mature fiction, so that we can say its images are Gnostic but not its program, since it lacks all program. A Gnosticism without potential transcendence is the most negative of all possible negative stances, and doubtless accounts for the sympathetic reader's sense that every crucial work by Beckett necessarily must be his last. Yet the grand paradox is that lessness never ends in Beckett.

"Nothing is got for nothing." That is the later version of Emerson's law of compensation, in the essay "Power," in *The Conduct of Life*. Nothing is got for nothing even in Beckett, this greatest master of nothing. In the progression from *Murphy* through *Watt* and the trilogy on to *How It Is* and the briefer fictions of recent years, there is loss for the reader as well as gain. The same is true of the movement from *Godot, Endgame,* and *Krapp's Last Tape* down to the short plays of Beckett's current and perhaps final phase. A wild humor abandons Beckett, or is transformed into a comedy for which we seem not to be ready. Even an uncommon reader can long for those marvelous Pythagoreans, Wylie and Neary, who are the delight of *Murphy,* or for the sense of the picturesque that makes a last stand in *Molloy.* Though the mode was Joyce's, the music of Wylie and Neary is Beckett's alone:

> "These are dark sayings," said Wylie.
> Neary turned his cup upside down.
> "Needle," he said, "as it is with the love of the body, so with the friendship of the mind, the full is only reached by admittance to the most retired places. Here are the pudenda of my psyche."
> "Cathleen," cried Wylie.
> "But betray me," said Neary, "and you go the way of Hippasos."
> "The Adkousmatic, I presume," said Wylie. "His retribution slips my mind."
> "Drowned in a puddle," said Neary, "for having divulged the incommensurability of side and diagonal."
> "So perish all babblers," said Wylie.
>   . . . . .
> "Do not quibble," said Neary harshly. "You saved my life. Now palliate it."
> "I greatly fear," said Wylie, "that the syndrome known as life is too diffuse to admit of palliation. For every symptom that is eased, another is made worse. The horse leech's daughter is a closed system. Her quantum of wantum cannot vary."
> "Very prettily put," said Neary.

One can be forgiven for missing this, even as one surrenders these easier pleasures for the more difficult pleasures of *How It Is*:

> my life above what I did in my life above a little of everything tried everything then gave up no worse always a hole a ruin always a crust never any good at anything not made for that far-

rago too complicated crawl about in corners and sleep all I
wanted I got it nothing left but go to heaven

The sublime mode, according to a great theorist, Angus
Fletcher, has "the direct and serious function of destroying the
slavery of pleasure." Beckett is certainly the strongest living
Western author, the last survivor of the sequence that includes
Proust, Kafka, Joyce. It seems odd to name Beckett, most astonishing of minimalists, as a representative of the sublime
mode, but the isolation and terror of the high sublime return
in the catastrophe creations of Beckett, in that vision Fletcher
calls "catastrophe as a gradual grinding down and slowing to a
dead stop." A sublime that moves toward silence necessarily
relies upon a rhetoric of waning lyricism, in which the entire
scale of effects is transformed, as John Hollander notes: "Sentences, phrases, images even, are the veritable arias in the plays
and the later fiction. The magnificent rising of the kite at the
end of *Murphy* occurs in a guarded but positive surge of cere-
monial song, to which he will never return."

Kafka's Hunter Gracchus, who had been glad to live and
was glad to die, tells us: "I slipped into my winding sheet like a
girl into her marriage dress. I lay and waited. Then came the
mishap." The mishap, a moment's error on the part of the
death ship's pilot, moves Gracchus from the heroic world of
romance to the world of Kafka and of Beckett, where one is
neither alive nor dead. It is Beckett's peculiar triumph that he
disputes with Kafka the dark eminence of being the Dante of
that world. Only Kafka, or Beckett, could have written the
sentence in which Gracchus sums up the dreadfulness of his
condition: "The thought of helping me is an illness that has to
be cured by taking to one's bed." Murphy might have said
that; Malone is beyond saying anything so merely expres-
sionistic. The "beyond" is where Beckett's later fictions and

plays reside. Call it the silence, or the abyss, or the reality beyond the pleasure principle, or the metaphysical or spiritual reality of our existence at last exposed, beyond further illusion. Beckett cannot or will not name it, but he has worked through to the art of representing it more persuasively than anyone else. He too beholds, with Wallace Stevens, "a way of truth," if not a way of meaning, a trope revealing that "Our bloom is gone. We are the fruit thereof."